2-50

5,000 ONE AND TWO LINERS
FOR ANY AND EVERY OCCASION

The one-liners and two-liners in this book have been specially selected from among the best of the author's collection of more than a million great jokes.

This book is devoted to all people who enjoy and appreciate a good gag or pun, and especially to my wife Fini, who spent endless hours watching me at work at my typewriter.

5,000
ONE AND TWO LINERS FOR ANY AND EVERY OCCASION

by

LEOPOLD FECHTNER

A. THOMAS AND COMPANY
Wellingborough, Northamptonshire

First published in the United Kingdom 1979

Original American edition published by
Parker Publishing Company, West Nyack, New York

ISBN 0 85454 064 4

Made and Printed in Great Britain by
Weatherby Woolnough, Wellingborough
Northants, England, NN8 4BX

How You Can Use This Book to Add Wit to Any and Every Occasion

Here are a few words on how you can get the most effective results from this book — the biggest assembly of one-liners and two-liners ever compiled. This book contains more than 5,000 items, sorted under 250 popular topics in alphabetical order, with an extensive Reference Guide which makes it possible to find one-liners or two-liners on any subject easily.

These days, people like humor that is quick and snappy; they like jokes that get to the point fast. These are the kinds of jokes in this book.

It was compiled not only to make *you* laugh, but to help you entertain other people. If you will open this book at random every morning, pick out a few one-liners or two-liners and memorize them, you will soon be known as a funny person everybody wants to meet. With a little practice, you'll find yourself remembering these short jokes without any effort. You'll surprise your family, your friends, and your business associates with your ready wit, and your ability to brighten discussion with a few quips will soon make you the center of every party you attend.

You are likely to get ahead faster on your job, make more sales, or get people to work harder for you, if you can add a bit of humor to the situation. You'll make everybody see things your way with funny lines.

Soon you may be asked to give little talks on particular subjects. Here's where this book is most helpful, because you can look up appropriate gags, either under the 250 popular topics in the Table of Contents, or if your subject is, by chance, not listed there, in the handy Reference Guide at the back, which will give you a rich variety of additional or connected gags.

For instance, many people are interested in travel, and someone may ask you to speak on this subject. You'll quickly find many good jokes listed under "Travel." Suppose, though, you want some additional gags about means of transportation; in the Reference Guide at the back you'll find: Aviation, Boats, Buses, Cars, Railroads and Taxis, and under each of these you'll find many funny lines.

The one-liners and two-liners in this book have been specially selected from among the best of the more than 1,000,000 great jokes in my unique "Humor Library," housed in The Museum of American Humor. From this spectacular storehouse of fun, top-flight professional humorists all over the country draw their material.

You'll chuckle as you read this book, but you'll get the most use out of it as you sprinkle a few of its gags into your daily discussions. There is nothing like the heartwarming satisfaction of making other people laugh.

KEEP SMILING!

Leopold Fechtner
Kew Gardens, N.Y.

A

Accidents

You look like an accident — waiting to happen.

The best way to avoid an automobile accident is to stay home on Sunday.

What an accident! I had the right of way but the other guy had the truck.

Every time my wife has an accident in the kitchen I get it for dinner.

He is so unlucky. He runs into accidents that started out happening to someone else.

Until the year 1957, I never had an accident. Then I bought a car.

If you get hurt crossing the street on the GREEN, does the RED CROSS pay for the BLUE CROSS?

He had a bad accident. He tried to fly his plane through a tunnel without checking the train schedules.

The best way to avoid a car accident is to travel by bus.

"How did the accident happen?"
"My wife fell asleep in the back seat of the car."

"How did you break your arm?"
"You see those porch stairs? I didn't."

"Did you ever have a car accident?"
"Well, I met my wife at a gas station."

"So your uncle fell down the stairs."
"Yes, but it was all the same: he wanted to come down anyway."

"How did you have this accident?"
"The sign said: STOP, LOOK, LISTEN! — and while I did the train hit me."

"How did you break your arm?"
"Trying to pat myself on my back for minding my own business."

"Have you ever been in an accident?"
"Yes. Once when I was on a train going through a tunnel, I kissed the father instead of his daughter."

"Mommy, Daddy just fell off the roof!"
"I know, dear; I saw him pass the window."

"How did you knock that man down on an empty road?"
"I didn't see him. My windshield is almost all covered with safety stickers."

Advice

Advice is something that most people take for a cold.

When good advice goes in one ear and out the other, it leaves a vacuum in between.

If you can tell the difference between good advice and bad advice, you don't need advice.

Always put your best foot forward, especially when walking in the dark.

When arguing with a stupid person, be sure he isn't doing the same.

The average bride gets enough advice to last her for several husbands.

If you are driving, make sure you have a car.

To avoid burning your hands in hot water, feel the water before putting your hands in.

The best cure for a hangover is to drink black coffee the night before instead of the morning after.

Tip for doctors: In case of amnesia, collect the fee in advance.

Advice to speakers: If you don't strike oil in the first two minutes you'd better stop boring.

If your child wants to lick the beaters on a mixer, shut off the motor before giving it to him.

Advice to people about to get married: Don't!

Advice to single girls; never look for a husband — look for a single man.

"My advice, sir, is to keep the oil and change the car!"

Advice is something everybody gives but few take.

Marry a woman with horse sense — she'll never nag.

When you drop ashes on the rug, spill a little of your martini to prevent fires.

To get a very soft boiled egg, just dip it in boiling water for a second.

The best time to buy a used car is when it's new.

The best time to miss a train is at a crossing.

Age

My uncle lived to be 100, and he owes it to mushrooms. He never ate them.

Her age is a millinery secret. She keeps it under her hat.

Few women admit their age. Few men act theirs.

My wife is now 60. I'll split two for one and get two 30s.

I knew her 40 years ago and she looked just like she looks today: Old.

Old? He chases his secretary around the desk, but can't remember why.

Old? His toupee turned gray.

Old? She still carries around a nickel for mad money.

Old? When you get past 80 you are a maintenance problem.

Old? He is at the age when all phone numbers in his little black book are doctors.

Old? She is approaching middle age for the third time.

Old? When he walks he creaks and when he talks he squeaks.

Old? He gets tired brushing his teeth.

Old? He dropped something on the floor and waited till he had to tie his shoelaces to pick it up.

She must be 28 years old. I counted the rings under her eyes.

The best age is marri-age.

The only thing worse than being old and bent is being young and broke.

A woman stops telling her age as soon as it starts telling on her.

One figure that's always on the up and up is a woman's estimate of her neighbor's age.

She holds her age well. She's been 28 for years.

There are some women who won't lie about their age — they just refuse to talk about it.

As a child I was very young.

Every woman tries to take a few years off her age and add it on to that of another woman.

After 45, your get-up and go has got-up and gone.

She told him he looked like a million and she meant every year of it.

30 is a nice age for a woman — especially if she happens to be 40.

He always remembers your age but always forgets your birthday.

"How old do you think I am?"
"You don't look it!"

"I admit I won't see 22 again."
"You wouldn't recognize it."

"I wish I had been born in the Dark Ages."
"So do I. You look terrible in the light."

"I don't look 35, do I?"
"No, but I bet you did when you were."

"Do you remember when you were born?"
"No, I was too young."

"She carries her age well, doesn't she?"
"She should. She's had years of experience."

"How old is your little sister?"
"She's last year's model."

"Isn't it remarkable how Alice keeps her years?"
"Yes, she hasn't changed them for ten years."

"To what do you attribute your old age?"
"The fact that I was born a long time ago."

"Did she tell you her age?"
"Partly."

"When I was born they fired a 21-gun salute."
"Too bad they missed."

Air-conditioning

This place is air-conditioned. In fact, I've never seen air in this condition.

We have an automatic air-conditioner. Every time the weather gets very hot it automatically breaks down.

What this country needs is a power mower that can be operated from an air-conditioned room.

With air-conditioning you don't have to wait for winter to catch a cold. You can have it all summer.

They have an up-to-date air-conditioner in this restaurant. The waiter waves the menu in front of your face.

He always drives with all the windows closed in the hottest weather to make believe his car is air-conditioned.

The best way to enjoy the summer is to turn the air-conditioner on and the TV set off!

I have five years full guarantee on my new air-conditioner — if I don't use it.

My repairman refused to come and fix my air-conditioner. Claims it was too hot in my apartment.

This place has a new type of air-conditioner. It's known as the Open Door Policy.

As soon as I gave my girl an air-conditioner she gave me the breeze.

Air conditioning is most useful during months that have no "R" in them.

"I heard your TV set brought you a lot of pleasure this summer."
"Yes. I swapped it for an air-conditioner."

Alimony

He who loves and runs away may still be the one who has to pay!

There are only two ways to avoid alimony: either stay single or stay married.

My wife keeps reminding me that her allowance isn't as big as her alimony would be.

If I don't pay alimony this month, can my wife repossess me?

Antiques

If it is hard to dust, it's probably an antique.

One man's junk is another man's rare antique.

I nearly got killed yesterday. I went to an antique shop and asked: "What's new?"

She was so old every time she went to an antique show someone tried to buy her.

Antiques are things one generation buys, the next generation gets rid of, and the following generation buys again.

An antique isn't always as old as it's cracked up to be.

I bid on every item at the auction last week — and didn't get caught once.

"I'm a well-known collector of antiques."
"I know. I've seen your wife."

"Why do you say that our baby is going to be an auctioneer some day?"
"He already has your expensive watch under the hammer."

Apartments

It's a nice little apartment — overlooking the rent.

The walls of our apartment are so thin, I once asked my wife a question and got four different answers.

The walls in our apartment are so thin that whenever my wife peels onions the people next door cry.

The best way to make the landlord paint your apartment is to move out.

I called my landlord and said my apartment had terrible acoustics, and he wrote back and said that he caught them all long before I moved in.

They call them high-rise apartments because the rent rises sky-high.

His new apartment has so many windows that he now gets cross-pollution.

Army — Navy

I was 5F during the last war. That's a single man with children.

I was a war baby. My parents took a look at me and started fighting.

I joined the navy to see the world and spent four years in a submarine.

Never lose your head in a battle. You won't have a place to put your helmet.

Army food is very tasty. I got out of the army ten years ago and I can still taste it.

All the time I was in the army my wife sent me nagging letters. I couldn't even enjoy the war in peace.

Then I opened an army surplus store, but nobody wanted to buy a surplus army.

The best way to stay out of the army is to join the navy.

He's such an egotist that he joined the navy so the world could see him.

I was on K.P. so much I got a medical discharge. Dishpan hands!

"Well, speak up! How do you want your uniform, too big or too small?"

She had a heart like the U.S. Army — open for all men between the ages of 18 and 35.

I was thrown out of the submarine service. I was caught sleeping with the windows open.

The draft board is the world's largest travel agency.

We had five famous generals: General Motors, General Electric, General Foods, General Mills, and General Nuisance.

"What were you in civilian life?"
"Happy, sir!"

"I'm a West Pointer."
"You look like an Irish Setter to me."

"How would you like to work on a submarine?"
"I wouldn't. I can't sleep with the windows closed."

"Did you enlist?"
"No, we had a tornado and I was caught in the draft."

"And how did you like living in an army tent?"
"Oh, I had no room to complain."

"I suppose you soldiers like wine, women and song?"
"No, we don't care for music."

"What is the worst month for soldiers?"
"A long March."

Art — Artists

A modern artist is one who throws paint on a canvas, wipes it off with a cloth and sells the cloth.

I painted her in oil because she has a face like a sardine.

He paints nothing but modern art. His model has the hiccups.

It's easy to recognize a modern painting. It's the one you can't recognize.

My aunt is a quick-change artist. She works in a maternity ward.

My uncle is also a quick-change artist. He works in a penny arcade.

It's easy to understand modern art. If it hangs on the wall, it's a painting. If you can walk around it, it's a sculpture.

An art school is a place for young girls to pass the time between high school and marriage.

When some girls pose for an artist, the first thing he draws is the studio curtain.

She just loves finger-painting. She painted one of them blue, the other red, another....

I'm a very good sculptor. In fact, I come from a long line of chiselers.

He is such a poor artist, the only thing he can draw properly is his bath.

Is he an artist? He couldn't even draw a curtain!

You're not supposed to enjoy modern art; it's made to be written and talked about, not looked at!

Modern art is like trying to follow the plot in a bowl of alphabet soup.

The best way to tell if a modern painting is completed is to touch it. If the paint is dry, it's finished.

Rembrandt painted 700 pictures and Americans have all 7,000 of them.

Modern art is when you buy a picture to cover a hole in the wall – and then decide the hole looks much better.

"We just bought a Rembrandt."
"How many cylinders?"

"What does an artist like to draw best?"
"His salary."

"Sculptors run in my family."
"Yes, someone told me your family was a bunch of chiselers."

"Is this one of your abstract paintings?"
"No, that's a mirror."

Aviation

I never travel by plane. The long trip to the airport makes me car-sick.

These new planes are so fast, you have to set the control for landing before taking off.

I even get air-sick when I lick an air-mail stamp.

Our plane had motor trouble, so we all got out and pushed.

People who fly look down on people who don't fly.

I have a fear of heights. Whenever I fly I ask the pilot to stay on the runway as long as possible.

Every year it takes less time to fly across the ocean and longer to drive to work.

I just flew in from Florida. Now my arms are tired.

I even get dizzy looking at an airplane ticket.

The runways are so long now, it took us longer to take off from the airport than it did to fly to Chicago.

I wouldn't say we were flying blind, but the instrument panel in the pilot's cabin was in braille.

Just as we were landing the stewardess asked us to fasten our belts. I was in trouble. I only wear suspenders.

No one has ever complained of a parachute not opening.

There's still a bit of risk in aviation — the taxi ride from the city to the airport.

Believe me, if you have to fly, go by plane!

This couple is so cautious they won't fly in the same plane. They even take separate escalators in stores.

This jet age can be defined as breakfast in London, lunch in New York, dinner in San Francisco, and baggage in Buenos Aires.

It will soon take only two hours to get around the world — one hour for the flying and one hour to get to the airport.

"I hate to be up there in a plane."
"I'd hate to be up there without one."

"This flight is sure bumpy."
"But sir, we didn't leave the runway yet!"

"Say, stewardess, why is the pilot laughing hysterically?"
"He's thinking of what they will say at the asylum when they find out he escaped."

"Look, the people way down there look like ants."
"They are ants. Our plane is still on the runway!"

"Who were the first men to make an airplane that didn't work?"
"The Wrong brothers."

"Can you telephone from an airplane?"
"Sure, anyone can tell a phone from an airplane."

"Do you have any experience in flying?"
"I fell out of a window once."

B

Babies

The best way to drive a baby buggy is to tickle his feet.

They said the baby looked like me. Then they turned him rightside up.

"Quick, bring the hammer. There's a fly on baby's head!"

When I was born everybody was so happy. Even the doctor said, "I think it's a baby!"

To me, every baby resembles every baby I ever saw.

Most babies born today are very young.

He's been hitting the bottle for years. He will be two tommorrow.

All babies are subject to change without notice.

Many a woman's mistakes are covered by a baby blanket.

We feed our baby onions so we can find it in the dark.

I was a premature baby. My father wasn't expecting me.

I'll never forget the day I was born. I cried like a baby.

I was such a big baby when I was born, the doctor was afraid to slap me.

We call our baby Teeny. We'd call him Martini but he isn't dry enough.

When I was born they didn't know whether to buy a crib or a cage.

Getting the baby to sleep is hardest when she's about 18 years old.

He used to be a bottle baby, but when he reached the age of ten he pushed the cork out and escaped.

If the baby doesn't go to sleep, lay him on the edge of the bed and he will drop off.

Our baby swallowed a pin, but it was all right. It was a safety pin.

"Honey, you'd better get up and see why the baby isn't crying!"

Our baby looks just like me. But it doesn't matter just as long as he's healthy.

We keep our baby on the phonograph because it has an automatic changer.

"Do you know, there's a baby born in New York every minute."
"Well, don't look at me that way. I live in Ohio!"

"This baby of mine might be a president."
"Whoever heard of a baby president?"

"What do you call your new baby?"
"Prince of Wails."

"Were there any great men born in this town?"
"No, only little babies."

"But Henry, that isn't our baby."
"Let's take it, it's a nicer carriage."

"We got a new baby in our house."
"What did you do with the old one?"

"I heard you got a new baby in your house."
"I don't think he's new. The way he cries shows he's had a lot of experience."

"When the baby cries at night, who gets up?"
"The whole neighborhood."

"Is your husband helping you with the baby?"
"Sure. Right now he's taking a nap for the baby."

"Who is bigger, Mr. Bigger or his baby?"
"The baby is a little Bigger."

"Is your baby a boy or a girl?"
"Of course, what else could it be?"

"Come over to our house; we have a new baby."
"That's nothing. We have a new Daddy."

"Where is the baby?"
"In the bawl pen."

Babysitters

Your babysitter just called. She wants to know where you keep the fire extinguisher.

Then I was offered a job as a babysitter. But who wants to sit on babies?

Babysitters tell me a good way to keep a child quiet is to let him suck on a bottle of glue.

An absent-minded babysitter put the TV to bed and watched the baby.

Is she hungry? She eats like a babysitter!

Bachelors

Many a poor husband was once a rich bachelor.

Show me a man who does what he wants, and I'll show you a bachelor

Not all men are fools. Some are bachelors.

A man calls himself a bachelor until he gets married. Then you should hear what he calls himself.

There are four ways for a bachelor to remain happy: North, South, East and West.

A man who refused to fight used to be called a coward. Now they call him a bachelor.

Never believe a fellow who says he is single unless he can show you his pay envelope on Monday.

To a bachelor a wedding ring is just a tourniquet. It stops circulation.

Banks — Banking

My bank just sent me a letter telling me it's the last time they will spend eight cents to tell me I have two cents in my account.

They turned me down for a travel loan. I only wanted enough money for a one-way ticket to Europe.

My friend wants to work in a bank. He thinks there is money in it.

My wife and I have a joint account. I deposit and she draws it.

If money doesn't grow on trees, why do banks have so many branches?

The man who writes the bank's advertising is not the man who makes the loans.

This bank is so big, they even have a special window for hold-ups.

A banker may write a bad poem and get away with it; but just let a poet try to write a bad check.

My wife had an accident at the bank recently. She got in the wrong line and made a deposit.

Joint accounts prove that many wives are quick on the draw.

My brother ran the Chase National Bank for years. Now the bank runs a national chase for him.

He is so small they offered him a job in a piggy bank.

The only man who counts in this world is a bank cashier.

When a draft passes through a bank, does it give the clerk a cold?

She was built like the First National Bank — everything deposited in the right places.

A joint checking account is never overdrawn by the wife. It is just under-deposited by her husband.

Every time I overdraw my checking account the bank president comes to my house and takes away the calendar.

Even my bank tries to save money now. Their latest calendar has only six months.

If the bank in Red Bank, New Jersey buys the bank in Long Branch, New Jersey it will be called: The Long Branch branch of the Red Bank bank.

The new drive-in bank permits a husband to deposit from the front seat while his wife withdraws from the back seat.

"Did they catch the man who robbed the bank?"
"No, but they caught three people who didn't."

"Miss Jones, do you retire a loan?"
"No, sir, I sleep with my aunt."

"What is the name of your bank?"
"Piggy."

"I'd go through anything for you."
"Let's start with your bank account."

"Did you get the check I sent you?"
"Twice — once from you and once from the bank."

"Your bank account is overdrawn."
"Well, maybe all my checks aren't in yet."

"You're looking for a bank cashier? Didn't you hire one yesterday?"
"That's the one we are looking for."

"Can you describe the missing cashier?"
"Sure. He is five feet tall and $7,000 short."

"Why are you putting that calendar in your piggy bank?"
"Because I want to save time!"

"My bank just told me my account is overdrawn again."
"Try some other bank. They can't all be overdrawn."

"The bank has returned your check."
"Fine. What can we buy with it now?"

Barbers — Barbershops

I wanted to get a haircut, but they were all out of them.

He gives a lousy haircut, but he knows all the latest stories.

He has such a long face the barbers charge him twice for shaving.

Would you say a barber is one who talks behind your back?

The way hair styles are today, you can't tell from the back if it is a man who needs a haircut or a woman who just had one.

"Just a shave, please, I haven't got the time to listen to a haircut!"

When one barber cuts another barber's hair, which one does the talking?

"Sir, I just hope your tie was red when you came in."

My barber is an authority on everything except how to cut hair.

"Do you shave yourself all the time?"
"No, I stop occasionally for food."

"Why did you drop the hot towel on my face?"
"Did you think I was going to burn my fingers?"

"You say your wife caused you to grow that long beard?"
"Yes, she started buying my neckties."

"How do you want your hair cut?"
"Off!"

"I know a man who takes his hat off to nobody."
"How does he get a haircut?"

"Are you the man who cut my hair the last time?"
"No sir, I've only worked here for a year."

"You say you have been in my barbershop before. I don't remember your face."
"Oh, it's all healed up now."

Bartenders

What a bartender! I asked for a stiff drink and he put cement in my beer.

Please, bartender, put two cherries in my Manhattan. My doctor told me I should eat more fruit.

What a bartender! When I asked him for something tall, cold and full of gin, he called his wife out!

The new bar now has three bartenders — two for serving and one for listening.

Now the bartenders are asking for more overtime pay — time and a fifth.

"Talk to me, honey. Make believe I'm your bartender."

Some bartenders expect a 25-cent tip when they give you a $1 check for a 30-cent bottle of beer.

"Say, bartender, isn't it a beautiful day?"
"Did you come here to drink or to talk?"

"Do you serve women at this bar?"
"No, sir, you must bring your own."

"This brandy is one hundred years old."
"It is? It tastes just like new."

"Down south, we like our liquor hard and our women soft."
"Well, here, we like our liquor straight and the women curved."

Baseball

We went to a baseball party. That's one where all the bases are loaded.

This baseball player was so kind, they had to fire him. He wouldn't even hit a fly.

If you want to see a baseball game in the worst way — take your wife along.

My girl is a real athlete. Always ready to play ball with me.

I always get the same seat at the ball park — between the hot dog vendor and his best customer.

Ballplayers will never have a union. After all, no ballplayer wants to be called out on strikes.

Another rare sight is a man trying to get to first base with an old bat.

We call her 'Baseball' because she won't play without a diamond.

She calls her stockings 'Baseball' because they have three runs.

The best way to have nine men run after you is to play baseball.

Women are like baseball umpires. They make quick decisions, never reverse them, and they don't think you're safe when you're out.

"Yes, I know we have a man on every base, but so has the other side!"

Bathing

People who take cold baths all winter seldom have a cold — but they have cold baths.

My mother dropped my towel into the bathtub and now she dried me wetter than I was before.

I found myself on the Sahara Desert in a bathing suit. There wasn't any water, but what a beach!

Women's clothes are really crazy. My wife wears more when she takes a bath than when she takes a walk.

A bath is something you take when you find yourself in hot water.

When taking a bath he always puts cotton in his ears so he won't hear the ring around the tub.

They now have a new soap called "Third Degree." Makes you come clean.

They call this new soap "Boo." It scares the dirt away.

Don't ever go into water after a hearty meal. You'll never find it there.

The only thing that will make a pretty girl scream while taking a bath is to discover that there are three hands washing her back.

He got a medal for bravery on the beach. Rescued a girl from a life-guard.

Cold baths are more enjoyable when taken with hot water.

I'm using a square bathtub so I can't get a ring.

He is so honest, he worked in a Turkish Bath for two years and never took a bath.

I now have a bathtub in my livingroom, so when the doorbell rings I don't have far to walk.

There is a new soap on the market. It doesn't clean, it doesn't lather, it doesn't bubble. Just company in the tub.

My doctor told me to take a bath before retiring. But the way business is going I won't be able to retire for twenty years.

This morning I had water on the knee, water on the elbow, and water on the brain. Then I turned off the shower.

This new soap not only floats — if you whistle it swims over to you.

Every time I took a bath my phone rang. So I complained to the phone company and they came and took away my bathtub.

I was going to give her a bathrobe. But I know that she wouldn't want to bathe a robe.

I wanted to give her something she needs but I don't know how to wrap up a bath.

Does he take a bath? They had to burn the house down to get him out of the tub.

Every evening I stay under the shower for five minutes and once a week I turn the water on.

Every morning I take a cold shower. I have grapefruit for breakfast.

Some days I have to take three or four baths to make the phone ring.

A man who crosses the ocean twice without taking a bath is a dirty double-crosser!

Speaking of bathing in famous springs — I bathed in the spring of 1938.

My doctor said I should bathe in milk but I couldn't get into the bottle.

Many a bathing girl has gotten into deep water.

My uncle takes a bath every week, whether he needs it or not.

"Do you exercise after a morning bath?"
"Yes, I usually step on the soap as I get out."

"What made you leave the boardinghouse after three years?"
"I found out they had no bathtub."

"What color bathing suit was she wearing?"
"I couldn't see. She had her back turned."

"My wife ran away while I was taking a bath."
"I'll bet she waited years for the opportunity."

"Did you take a bath?"
"Why? Is there one missing?"

"Do you like bathing beauties?"
"I don't know. I never bathed any."

"Can you give me a room with a bath?"
"I can give you the room but you have to take your own bath!"

"Come out of the water, there's no bathing allowed here!"
"But officer, I'm not bathing. I'm drowning!"

"Madam, do you wish a room with a private bath?"
"Yes, that's the only kind I care to take."

"How did mother find out you didn't take a bath?"
"I forgot to wet the soap."

"Did you drink carrot juice after a hot bath?"
"No, doctor. I haven't finished the bath yet."

"Do you always bathe in muddy water?"
"It wasn't muddy when I got in."

Bathing Suits

She wore a bathing suit that fit like a sunburn.

She is so modest, she just bought a bathing suit with sleeves.

When a girl has nothing on her mind she is thinking of her bathing suit.

The less there is to a woman's bathing suit, the more it costs.

Does she have fancy bathing suits? They are all marked: Dry Clean Only!

Some of the bathing suits look like they haven't been delivered yet.

The new bathing suits don't shrink. They have no place to shrink to.

She bought a bikini that's smaller than the pricetag.

To wear a bikini a girl must have the figure or the nerve.

Bathing suits today are really something — if you can call nothing something.

She's one of those girls who asks for very little, especially when buying a bathing suit.

Some girls think those new bathing suits are indecent. Others have good figures.

A girl who pays a lot for a bathing suit will have little to show for it.

A bathing beauty these days wears nothing to speak of, but plenty to talk about.

The Beach

A place at the seashore where people lie about how rich they are in town.

A place where a girl goes in her baiting suit.

A place where people slap you on the back and ask you how you're peeling.

A place where a woman goes nowadays when she has nothing to wear.

A place where women reveal their figures and conceal their ages.

The girls on this beach are so attractive, even the tide refused to go out.

We call our cabana "Co-Co." Now we can say: "Let's have lunch in our Cococabana!"

We spent all day on the sundrenched beach, but it was so cold we came home with frostbitten suntans.

The resort was so dull, one day the tide went out and never came back.

"Was it hot on the beach today?"
"Terrible! It was so hot we took turns sitting in each other's shadows."

"Did you know I was a lifesaver last summer?"
"Really, what flavor?"

"So, the lifeguard is teaching you how to swim. What have you learned so far?"
"That he's single and has a good job."

Beauty

She has calves that only a cow could love.

A woman's best beauty aid is a near-sighted man.

A beauty is a girl who has a lovely profile all the way down.

Her figure is harder to ignore than a ringing telephone.

If I told you that you have a beautiful body would you hold it against me?

Today a girl can be pretty as a picture, providing she's well-painted.

Beauty is what a woman has when when she looks the same after washing her face.

If you want to be a stand-out beauty, mingle with ugly people.

"She is the ugliest girl I ever saw."
"Dear, you forgot yourself."

"My girl has lots of personality."
"Mine isn't good looking either."

"May I see you pretty soon?"
"Don't you think I'm pretty now?"

"Was that your wife who let me in?"
"Who else? Would I hire a maid that homely?"

"She sure is a striking beauty."
"You said it! She slapped me twice."

"Mother, what is gray hair a sign of?"
"That the beautician is on vacation."

"That girl is certainly the picture of health."
"Yes, she's mighty well painted."

"Sir, did the mudpack help your wife's appearance?"
"It did for a few days, but then it fell off."

"Why are beautiful women like bread?"
"Because they are always toasted."

"Are the girls in your town pretty?"
"Well, let me put it this way; we held a beauty contest and nobody won."

"I told my girl she looked like the breath of spring."
"No, you didn't say that. You said she looked like the end of a hard winter."

"Next to a beautiful girl, what do you consider the most interesting thing in the world?"
"When I'm next to a beautiful girl I don't give a damn about statistics."

Every time I meet a beautiful girl either she is married or I am.

The best way to fill out a pink slip is with a beautiful body.

A thing of beauty keeps you broke forever.

If you think she's beautiful you ought to see her photographs.

"Darling, you look wonderful. What happened?"

Since I told her she has a nice profile, she's trying to walk sideways.

Her figure? She looks more like a bottle of milk than a bottle of coke.

The best way for a girl to make herself beautiful is to give her boyfriend a couple of drinks.

The better a woman looks, the longer a man does.

After a few drinks every woman looks beautiful.

Her face, figure, and voice makes you stop, look, and listen.

"You're pretty dirty, Sally."
"Yes, and I'm even prettier when I'm clean."

"My husband calls me the best looking girl in the world."
"My husband has bad eyesight, too."

"What has she got that I haven't got?"
"Shall I give it to you alphabetically?"

"Do you think I will lose my looks as I get older?"
"I hope you'll be that lucky."

The Beauty Parlor

"I've just come from the beauty parlor."
"Too bad they were closed."

"You are a hairdresser. What do you have for gray hair?"
"The greatest respect, madam."

"You said your mother is dying and I just saw her at the beauty parlor."
"That's where she's dying. She's going to be a blonde now."

She goes to the beauty parlor on Monday and comes back on Wednesday.

She goes to the beauty parlor to get a faceful of mud and an earful of dirt.

She spends three hours weekly at the beauty parlor, just to get an estimate!

It's an ill wind that blows the minute you leave the beauty parlor.

She got one of those poodle haircuts. Looks like a new man.

She goes to the only beauty parlor that never lives up to its name.

My wife found a beauty parlor that has a recovery room.

If my wife stays away from her beauty parlor for one week she doesn't know what's going on in the neighborhood.

Lots of women still believe in miracles. If you don't think so, just visit a beauty parlor.

Bills

Bills are something that some people have trouble meeting but most people have trouble dodging.

Some people pay their bills when due, some when overdue, and some never do.

My wife brings more bills into the house than a Congressman.

Birds

A bird in hand can be an awful mess.

A bird in hand is bad table manners.

A bird in hand is worthless when you want to blow your nose.

My wife does bird imitations. She always watches me like a hawk.

"Hi, birdie, can you talk?"
"Yeah, I can talk. Can you fly?"

"I spent ten dollars on a canary yesterday."
"That's nothing. I spent fifty on a lark."

"You say it's $2.50 for the cage and only $3.00 all together?"
"Yes, you see, I'm giving you the bird."

Birthdays

My folks can never forget my birthday. I was born between the second payment on the radio and the sixth on the car.

He always remembers his wife's birthday. It's the day after she reminds him of it.

"For weeks I've been telling you not to buy anything for my birthday and you still forgot to bring me something."

When a man has a birthday he takes a day off, but when a woman has a birthday she takes a year off.

We were so poor we couldn't give my sister a sweet-16 party until she was 28.

He was born on April 2nd — a day too late.

She was born in the year of our Lord only knows.

He always remembers your age but forgets your birthday.

He was born with a silver spoon in his mouth and hasn't stirred since.

Her 30th birthday isn't far away — only about six years ago.

I was born on the first of the month so they called me "Bill."

My wife just got a mink coat. She gave it to herself for my birthday.

She's celebrating the 25th anniversary of her 28th birthday.

I was so surprised at my birth, I couldn't talk for a year and a half.

My wife gave me a wonderful birthday present. She let me win an argument.

A man who forgets his wife's birthday will get something to remember her by.

The best way to remember your wife's birthday is to forget it once.

He was born with a silver spoon in his mouth and every time he goes to a restaurant he tries to complete the set.

I think he was born upside down. His nose runs and his feet smell.

"Say, could you put "Happy Birthday" on this pizza?"

"Happy birthday, Honey! What is it like to be 30 for the second time around?"

You're getting old when the only thing you want for your birthday is not to be reminded of it.

It is sure terrible to grow old alone — my wife hasn't had a birthday in four years.

Did she give me a surprise on my last birthday! She got up and made breakfast.

"I was sure you would forget my birthday so I bought myself this fur coat."

A well-adjusted woman is one who not only knows what she wants for her birthday, but even knows what she's going to exchange it for.

"I was born in vain."
"That's funny. I was born in Chicago."

"How come you were born in Iowa?"
"I wanted to be near my mother."

"What sign were you born under?"
"A delicatessen sign."

"I hate to think of my 29th birthday."
"Why? What happened?"

"I'm looking forward to my 23rd birthday."
"You're facing in the wrong direction."

"Are you coming to my 18th birthday party?"
"No, I went to that one five years ago."

"I celebrated my 23rd birthday yesterday."
"What, again?"

"Tomorrow I celebrate my 24th birthday."
"Well, better late than never."

"When is your birthday? I want to buy you a present."
"You're way late. I was born many years ago."

"In what state were you born?"
"In the nude."

"A funny thing happened to my mother in New York."
"I thought you were born in Chicago?"

"Oh, my! Something terrible has just happened."
"What? Did they find your birth certificate?"

Birthday Cakes

By the time the last candle was lit on her birthday cake, the first one had gone out.

She had so many candles on her last birthday cake every guest got a sunburn.

At the birthday party I tried to count the candles but the heat drove me back.

She had so many candles on her cake the air-conditioning couldn't be felt.

There were so many candles she barbecued the ceiling.

But she is very economical. She had only 26 candles on her 40th birthday cake.

"Honey, looking at those candles, I must say you are getting younger every year!"

If she ever told her real age her birthday cake would be a fire hazard.

Well, I see, this is sure a surprise party. Only 32 candles on your cake!

The design on a woman's birthday cake is often beautiful, but the arithmetic is usually terrible.

It's a good thing she celebrates her birthday in the winter because the candles heat up the whole house.

She had so many candles on her birthday cake she was fined for air pollution.

She tried to bake a birthday cake but the candles melted in the oven.

When she lit all candles on her birthday cake three people collapsed from the heat.

There were so many candles on her last birthday cake they melted the cake.

Her last birthday cake looked like a prairie fire.

She needed ten matches to light her last birthday cake.

She needs a fire permit to put the candles on her birthday cake.

Blood

They asked me to be a blood donor. I'm not even a blood owner.

I went down to the blood bank but they turned me down. They want plasma, not asthma.

The next time I went to the blood bank they said they couldn't use me, but if they ever need hot water they'll call me.

He went to the pier looking for blood vessels.

He stayed up all night studying for a blood test.

Boats

There was a little tugboat that committed suicide when it discovered that its mother was a tramp and its father was a ferry.

You think you have trouble? What about the deep-sea diver coming up, who passed his ship going down?

I like to run my home like a ship with me as a captain. Too bad I married an admiral.

It takes about two days at sea to make some travelers look like their passport photograph.

Her family is very exclusive. They didn't come over on the Mayflower — they had their own boat.

Every time I get on a ferry it makes me cross.

When your ship finally comes in you will usually find relatives waiting at the dock.

He calls his boat "Canasta" because it has two decks.

Men go on cruises for the fishing, girls go on cruises for the hunting.

I can row — canoe?

She waited so long for her dreamboat to come in her pier collapsed.

"They have just dropped the anchor."
"I was afraid they would. It was dangling there all day."

"Oh, steward, I've got a complaint. A sailor peeked into my cabin."
"Well, what do you expect in second class, the captain?"

"Quick, operator, send an S. O. S.!"
"How do you spell it?"

"How was your boat ride yesterday?"
"He not only lied about the size of his yacht, he made me row!"

"Say, captain, isn't the boat a day behind schedule?"
"Oh, we don't worry about little things. We're glad if it isn't sinking."

"I put all our clothes in that little closet with the glass window."
"You dope! That's the port hole!"

"Do boats sink often?"
"Only once!"

"Should this boat sink, whom would you save first, me or the children?"
"Me."

"You were the only survivor of the shipwreck. How come?"
"I missed the boat."

"Say, captain, I misplaced my lifesaver, could I have another one?"
"We are all out of them, but here, have a coughdrop."

"And what did you do when the boat sank in mid-ocean?"
"Oh, I just grabbed a cake of soap and washed myself ashore."

Books

Every time I read a book some pages are missing.

Most people read books. He reads gas meters.

Every time I lend him a book, he keeps it. He's a professional bookkeeper.

Never give a person a book for a gift. He may already have one.

My problem is that it takes me six weeks to read the Book of the Month.

I can read her like a book, but I keep forgetting my place.

Never judge a book by its movie.

I have a hundred books, but no bookcase. Nobody will lend me a bookcase.

I just finished my first book and next year I'm going to read another one.

Some of today's movies are so long, it takes less time to read the book.

By the time a man can read women like a book he's too old to start a library.

The only book that really tells you where you can go on vacation is your checkbook.

Yes, you can read her like a book if you care for that type of literature.

I didn't mind when he kept borrowing my books, but when he asked to borrow my bookcase I hit him.

I'm reading a very unusual murder mystery. Seems the victim was shot by a man from another book.

There are so few books in our house that if the TV set breaks down, we'll have to talk to each other.

To keep your library intact, buy three copies of each book — one to show, one to loan and one to read.

"Are you an avid reader?"
"I don't know. I never read Avid."

"Is your husband a bookworm?"
"No, just an ordinary one."

"I read your new book. Who wrote it for you?"
"Who read it to you?"

"It took me a whole year to write a book."
"Stupid. You can buy one for 50 cents."

"What book do you like best?"
"My husband's checkbook."

"What is black and white and red all over?"
"A book."

"Did you ever read a book by Shakespeare?"
"No, but I read a book by candlelight."

"How may bookkeeping be taught in three words?"
"Never lend them."

"How did you like my book?"
"It was good, but too long in the middle."

"I'd like to buy a book — something very deep."
"How about 20,000 Leagues Under The Sea?"

"We have a book in our family for 50 years."
"Isn't it about time you returned it?"

"Have you read Shakespeare?"
"No, but I have red pajamas."

Bowling

Interest your children in bowling. Get them off the streets and into the alleys.

Bowling is the second most popular indoor sport.

Bowling is a sport that should be right down your alley.

If you don't hear a pin drop, then something is wrong with your bowling.

Boxing

He was a colorful fighter – black and blue all over.

Every morning I shadow box. Today I won, after ten minutes.

When the fight ended I was smiling from ear to ear – no teeth.

When the fight ended I was handed a cup – to keep my teeth in.

A knockout is something that happens when a boxer makes short work of his job.

Marriage is a lot like boxing. Sometimes the preliminaries are better than the main event.

Then, there is the boxing club that chose black and blue as its club colors.

A boxer is a man who makes money hand over fist.

He is probably the best fighter in the country, but he always gets beat in the city.

"Have I done him any damage?"
"Not yet, but keep on swinging. The draft might give him a cold."

"What should a prize fighter drink?"
"Punch."

Bridge

I have a bridge date tonight, but I can't remember if it's the Brooklyn or George Washington.

It's not a sin to play bridge, but it's a crime the way some people play it!

About the only time the average husband and wife get enjoyment out of holding hands is when they are playing bridge.

If looks could kill, a lot of people would die with bridge cards in their hands.

Bridge is a game of cards in which a good deal depends upon a good deal.

A women's bridge club is a place where women go to giggle, gab, gobble, and gamble.

It's amazing what fine poker hands I get when I play bridge.

Most women don't play bridge skillfully, but they always play fluently.

Bridge is a friendly game invented by two married couples who disliked each other.

"How is your headache, Bill?"
"Out playing bridge."

"Does your wife play bridge for money?"
"She does, but she never gets any."

"Shall we have a friendly game of cards?"
"No, let's play bridge."

"How did you like the bridge party last night?"
"Fine, until the cop looked under the bridge."

"What kind of bridge does your wife play?"
"Judging by the cost, I'd say it was a toll bridge."

"It takes two to make a quarrel."
"No, Mother, you need four to play bridge."

"I heard you taught your wife how to play bridge."
"Yes, and last week I won back half my salary."

Brides

She is walked to the altar so often, they're trying to make her pay for the carpet.

The bride didn't look happy, she looked triumphant.

She's taken so many trips to the altar, the last time she went blindfolded.

"Poor girl! Always a bride — never a bridesmaid!"

Did you hear about the bride who was so ugly everybody kissed the bridesmaid?

I heard that every time a bride gets a shower, her groom gets soaked.

She's been married so often that wedding bells sound like an alarm clock to her.

The only time you can see a blushing bride nowadays is when the groom doesn't show up.

They wanted to give her a shower but they couldn't drag her into the bathroom.

There are a few four-letter words that will shake up every bride — like cook, wash, dust and iron.

They say all brides are beautiful. So where do the homely women come from?

She is a May-bride. She may or may not get married.

Why does a bride always look stunning, and the groom stunned?

"I heard you stopped taking out Helen."
"Yes, she began to have bride ideas."

"Here is a picture of my bride."
"She must be very wealthy."

"Do you remember the time I was a blushing bride?"
"No, dear, I didn't attend your first wedding."

"Have you kissed the bride?"
"No, not lately."

Budgets

So much of my money goes to balance the budget, I don't have any budget to balance.

My wife just balanced our budget. She cut herself down to 15 phone calls.

The time to start economizing is before you run out of money.

A budget is usually made up of a little money and a lot of estimates.

My wife told me that she finally worked out our budget — but one of us has to stop eating.

We figured out our budget just perfect. The money we owe is the same amount we had spent.

Buses

There's nothing faster on a takeoff than a bus you've just missed.

The new interstate buses are bigger than most of the towns they pass through.

I wouldn't say the bus was crowded, but even the driver was standing.

I was really insulted today. A bus driver asked me to move to the rear of the bus and the bus was empty.

The bus wasn't *too* crowded. I had a strap all to myself.

The buslines now have timetables, but it is against the rules for a bus to leave on time — this would upset the whole schedule.

Every time I get on a bus it's not going my way.

The best way to get a seat on a bus is to become a bus driver.

"I just hope you're getting off soon, because you are standing on my foot."

He took the bus home after work but his mother made him take it back.

He became a bus driver so he could tell people where to get off.

He got off the bus backwards because he heard they were going to grab his seat.

I took the bus to Kansas and I was scared to death. I never drove a bus before.

The bus was so crowded even some of the men couldn't get seats.

You can always find an empty seat on a bus going in the wrong direction.

"How old are you, little girl?"
"If you don't mind, driver, I'll just pay full fare and keep my statistics to myself!"

"Why are you crossing the street when the sign says: DON'T WALK?"
"Oh, I thought that was an ad from the bus company."

"It's too far to walk; why don't you take the bus home?"
"My parents wouldn't like it. We have a small house."

"Which end of the bus is the best one to get off?"
"It makes no difference — both ends stop."

"What are people who ride the Greyhound buses called?"
"Passengers."

"Driver, does this bus stop at the river?"
"If not, there's going to be a big splash."

"Say, driver, why does this bus stop at every corner?"
"Because it's a Greyhound, lady."

"So sorry, driver, but I'm afraid my little son has swallowed the ticket."
"Then I suggest, madam, you buy him a second helping."

Business

"Where do you complain about the complaint department?"

This place is so busy, the bargain basement is on the third floor.

I went to a dime store. They had a sale — two dimes for a quarter.

A sale is a place where a woman will ruin a $35 dress to get a house dress for $2.95.

Business is so bad that even the shoplifters have stopped coming.

A filing cabinet is a place where you can lose anything systematically.

"How did you do it? You've been here only two weeks and you're already two months behind in your work!"

"Are you really going to quit or are you just saying it to brighten my day?"

We can't fire her. She's the only one who understands the filing system.

Then we opened a branch office, but it was a flop. Nobody wanted to buy branches.

The big guns of business are usually those who have never been fired.

The boss is usually the only one who watches the clock during the coffee break.

Business is so quiet you can hear the overhead pile up.

I call my boss "Musketeer" because he always says I musketeer at 9 o'clock.

I call my boss "Morning" because he is always early.

A coal dealer is a man who does business on a large scale.

No customer can be worse than no customer.

People who sell perfume are always sticking their business in your nose.

To make a long story short, there's nothing like having the boss walk in.

"Sir, this price on the tag refers to city, state and federal taxes. The price of this merchandise is extra!"

When the office staff is having a picnic it may just mean that the boss is on vacation.

"Mr. Smith, this is just a suggestion. You don't have to do it unless you want to keep your job."

The most dangerous position in which to sleep is with your feet on your desk.

The boss said if my work doesn't improve he'll fire me. He can't, because I don't do anything.

A baker is a man who has his fingers in many pies.

Usually, business is very slow in the morning but it drops off in the afternoon.

"So you're Tom's boss! I've heard him mention your name so often, Mr. Slavedriver!"

Business is so good, I haven't the time to go to the bank to borrow money to pay my rent.

There's one sure way to make a businessman worry. Tell him not to.

I always laugh at my boss's jokes. It doesn't give me a lift, but it may get me a raise.

"Yes, Boss, I'm now saving my coffee breaks. When I get enough together I'm taking Friday off."

"I'm really not late, boss. I just took my coffee break before coming in!"

The worst thing about retirement is having to drink coffee on your own time.

I never agree with my boss until he says something!

"I heard you took an aptitude test."
"That's right, and they found out I'm best suited for retirement."

"What did the adding machine say to the clerk?"
"You can count on me!"

"Why do you go for a haircut on company time?"
"It grew on company time."

"So you're going to start a bakery?"
"Yes, if I can raise the dough."

"Young man, do you think you can handle a variety of work?"
"I ought to be able to. I've had 12 different jobs in four months."

"When is the best time to see the boss?"
"That's hard to say. Before lunch he's grouchy and after lunch he has indigestion."

"Was your boss sore when you told him you were quitting next week?"
"He sure was. He thought it was this week."

"One mousetrap, please, in a hurry. I have to catch a bus."
"Sorry, sir, our traps don't come that big."

"Why are you asking for a raise?"
"Well, boss, somehow my family found out that other people eat three meals a day."

"You should have been here at eight o'clock."
"Why, boss, what happened?"

"What is your business?"
"It's not business. It's a pursuit. I'm a bill collector."

"What business are you interested in?"
"Everybody's?"

"How's business?"
"Fifty-fifty. In the morning we get orders and in the afternoon they are cancelled."

"What does this mean? Someone just called up and said you were sick and couldn't come to work today?"
"Ha, Ha! The joke's on him, Boss. He was supposed to call tomorrow."

C

California

California is a fine place to live in, if you happen to be an orange.

California is a place where, when you drive less than 50 miles an hour, they consider you double-parked.

California is a place where it never rains. The sun just drips perspiration.

California is a place where saving up for rainy day is regarded as an insult.

California is so wonderful. On a clear day when the fog lifts, you can see the smog.

California is the only place where you can have all four seasons in one day.

Cars

My hubcaps keep coming off. Do you think there's too much air in the tires?

Driving while drunk is almost as dangerous today as walking while sober.

I once drove to California in six days. It took me four days to drive there and two days to refold the maps.

My wife is so emotional that she cries when a traffic light is against her.

Don't complain about the traffic. If there were fewer cars on the road it would be even harder to find a parking place.

"Say, I'm out of gas. Will it hurt my car if I drive with an empty tank?"

It's not a cheaper car that people want — it's an expensive car that costs less.

This man bought an electric car but could only go as far as Trenton. That's as far as the cord would reach.

I got a puncture in one tire. I didn't see the fork in the road.

My wife wanted a foreign convertible, so I bought her a rickshaw.

My new car has something that will last a lifetime — monthly payments.

Used cars are all right as far as they go.

Some joy rides extend from here to maternity.

A jay walker never knows where his next car is coming from.

A girl in a car is worth five in the phone book.

I was trying to get a new car for my wife but nobody would swap.

If your wife wants to learn how to drive, don't stand in her way.

The only time I suffer from car-sickness is when the payments are due.

It's a very economical car. Only uses oil when the motor is running.

The most dangerous part of a car is the nut that holds the steering wheel.

EVERY TIME I start my car it stalls.

EVERY TIME I find a parking space I have no dime.

EVERY TIME my car passes a junk yard it gets homesick.

EVERY TIME my car is in the middle of a car wash, the phone on the dashboard starts ringing.

EVERY TIME my wife finds an empty parking space she begs me to buy a car.

When it comes to used cars, it's hard to drive a bargain.

Don't play in the street – you may get that run down feeling.

A careful driver is one who just saw a driver ahead of him get a ticket.

Nothing improves your driving like a police car following you.

His car is for three people. One drives and two push.

It takes some people about three and a half cars to learn to drive.

The first thing that strikes a stranger in New York is a big car.

I used to be a safe driver but I gave it up. Who wants to drive a safe?

"Do you run a car?"
"No, I let the engine run it."

"Why did you park your car here?"
"The sign says: 'Fine for parking!'"

"How is your jalopy?"
"Oh, my wife is fine. How's yours?"

"What kind of a car do you have?"
"Pray as you enter!"

"Didn't you see the 25-mile per hour sign?"
"No, officer, I was driving too fast to see it."

"Has your wife learned to drive the car?"
"Only from the back seat."

"Is your car in good condition?"
"Sure, everything makes noise but the horn."

"Who was driving when you hit the pole?"
"Nobody, officer. We were all in the back seat."

"I just bought my wife a Rembrandt."
"So? Does she like sport cars?"

"Be careful how you drive. You almost went off the road."
"I thought you were driving."

"You certainly do keep your car nice and clean."
"It's an even deal. The car keeps me clean, too."

"Have you ever been car-sick?"
"Sure, every time my wife drives."

"My wife ran away with another man in my new car."
"Good Heavens? In your new car?"

"Did you save anything for a rainy day?"
"Yes, washing my car."

"I just bought a set of new balloon tires."
"Oh, I didn't know you had a balloon."

Cats

I fed some lemon to a cat and got a sour puss.

Even worse than raining cats and dogs is hailing taxis.

My cat can talk. I asked her what two minus two was and she said nothing.

A cat is an animal that never cries over spilled milk.

"You mustn't pull the cat's tail!"
"I'm only holding it. The cat is pulling!"

"Did you put the cat out?"
"Why? Is it on fire?"

"Your cat was making an awful noise last night."
"Yes, ever since she ate the canary she thinks she can sing."

"Name four animals of the cat family."
"The father cat, the mother cat and two kittens."

"Did you ever see the Catskill Mountains?"
"No, but I've seen them kill mice."

"Is it really bad luck to have a black cat following you?"
"Well, it depends on whether you're a man or a mouse."

"I heard you have a cat that can say her own name."
"Yes. Meow!"

Checks — Checkbooks

Every woman has a secret desire to write checks.

My wife loves to sign checks — on the back.

Don't count your checks before they are cashed.

I'm so underpaid I can't even cash my own check.

My wife acts very funny with a checkbook. Once she starts one, she can't put it down until it's finished.

"Honey, you always say I'm overdrawn. Did it ever occur to you that you might be under-deposited?"

My wife has a great sense of balance — except in her checkbook.

My wife sure loves checkbooks. Already finished 138 of them.

My wife calls our checking account the shrinking fund!

"But how can I be overdrawn when I still have 25 checks left?"

Chickens

Chickens are the only animals you can eat before they are born and after they are dead.

That rooster is so lazy, he waits for another rooster to crow, and then he nods his head.

Then there was the chicken who got sick. It had people pox.

This chicken lays eggs so big, it only takes six of them to make a dozen.

He keeps his chickens in a turning cement mixer. Now they are laying scrambled eggs.

Then he lets them swim around in a tub of hot water to lay hard-boiled eggs.

"What do you call a frightened skindiver?"
"Chicken of the Sea."

"What does a hen do when she stands on one foot?"
"Lifts up the other."

"On which side do chickens have the most feathers?"
"On the outside."

"How can you keep a rooster from crowing on Monday morning?"
"Eat him for Sunday dinner."

"Isn't this a good chicken?"
"It may have been good morally, but physically it's a wreck."

"How old was the chicken you just served me, waiter?"
"We don't furnish dates with chicken, sir, only bread and butter."

"Waiter, there's no chicken in the chicken soup."
"And you won't find any horse in the horseradish, either."

"Waiter, just look at that chicken. It's nothing but skin and bones!"
"Would you also like the feathers?"

"Are these eggs fresh?"
"Fresh? Why, the chickens haven't missed them yet."

"These are the best eggs we've had for years."
"Well, bring me some you haven't had so long."

"Be sure to make my eggs very soft-boiled."
Is it all right if I just carry them through a hot kitchen?"

"That's rather a small egg, isn't it?"
"Give it a chance. It was only laid yesterday."

Children

He is a fine broth of a boy. Too bad some of his noodles are missing.

As a child, I was the type of a kid my mother told me not to play with.

My kid shows signs of becoming an executive. Already he takes two hours for lunch.

Ever since he was eight years old, we've been pleading with our son to run away from home.

My son is now at the awkward age: too old to cry and too young to swear.

My son is now at the awkward age, too young for a credit card and too old for an allowance.

Just when your children get old enough that you can say you can stand them, they can't stand you.

The best way to keep children's clothes clean for several days is to keep them off the child.

My children are now at the perfect age. Too old to cry and too young to borrow the car.

She kept saying she wanted her children young. Who wants old children?

As a child I was sort of a cowboy. They used to say: "You're so fat, was your mother frightened by a cow, boy?"

Here is a child who is ready to run away from home, as soon as his parents get one.

"Ma! I managed to miss the schoolbus!"

My child eats dry toast and washes it down with crackers.

Youth is a wonderful thing. It's a crime that it's wasted on children.

Children should be seen and not had.

Today, children of six seem to know all the questions and at 16 they know all the answers.

Every family should have three children. If one turns out to be a genius, the other two can support him.

My children are finally grown up. My daughter started to put on lipstick and my son started to wipe it off.

She is his childhood sweetheart. When they married he was in his second childhood.

Most children eat spinach so they'll grow up big and strong enough to refuse it.

You can tell a child is growing up when he stops asking where he came from and starts refusing to tell where he is going.

I always help with the diapers. It's a good way to make a little change.

There's one thing about children – they never go around showing snapshots of their grandparents.

The little kid with the yo-yo said he could yo down, but he couldn't yo up again.

Buy the time a couple can really afford to have children, they're having grandchildren.

Children have become so expensive that only the poor can afford them.

They say children brighten up a home. That's right – they never turn off the lights.

He must get his brain from his mother. I still have mine.

As a child they kept him in the refrigerator – to keep him from getting spoiled.

If you wonder where your child left his roller skates, try walking around the house in the dark.

There's only one perfect child in all the world and every mother has it.

"Get Pop to tell you about the flowers and the bees! It's a riot!"

An allowance is what you pay your children to live with you.

"And what are you going to be if the neighbors let you grow up?"

"What's wrong, son?"
"I just had a fight with your wife!"

"Should women have children after 35?"
"No, 35 children are enough!"

"Darling, eat your spinach. It will put color in your cheeks."
"But, mom, who wants green cheeks?"

"Why is your little brother crying?"
"He just came down the stairs without walking."

"Henry, stop poking the baby."
"I'm not poking him, Ma, I'm counting his measles."

"I never told lies when I was a child."
"When did you begin, mother?"

"Are you a little boy or a little girl?"
"Sure, what else could I be?"

"Don't you want to grow up and be like Lincoln?"
"Who wants to be a tunnel?"

"John, how many times did I tell you not to play in the kitchen?"
"17 times, mother!"

"Say, madam, are all those children yours or is it a picnic?"
"They are all mine, conductor, and believe me, it's no picnic."

"What's all that racket you're making in the pantry, son?"
"I'm fighting temptation, mom."

"Why did you kick your little brother in the stomach?"
"He turned around."

"You shouldn't eat with your knife."
"But, Ma, my fork leaks!"

"Well, sonny, what's new in your house?"
"Who knows? They spell everything."

"But why did you put a frog into your sister's bed?"
"Because I couldn't find a mouse."

"You already have five children. Do you really like children so much?"
"No, but I just love to go to the PTA meetings."

Christmas

If it isn't too cold around Christmas time you have a cool Yule.

Santa Claus is the only man who shows some interest in an empty stocking.

A Santa Claus went to a psychiatrist and said: "Doc, I don't believe in myself!"

One store had two Santas. One had an express line for kids who ask for less than five toys.

Last year I explained to the children that there is no Santa Claus, and this year I'll try to explain it to my wife.

"Dear Santa, I want a plane, my bike fixed and my violin busted!"

An unemployed Santa Claus is a ho-ho hobo!

Sign in a big store: Five Santas, no waiting!

Christmas bills are the real mourning after.

"I'd like to join the Christmas Club but I don't have the time to attend the meetings."

I spent more than I meant to this Christmas. My wife exchanged her present for something more expensive.

Christmas brings the big question of where to pay how much for how many of which kind of what do give to whom.

Why don't women start wearing neckties so that men can get even with them at Christmas.

I didn't find any Christmas presents this year. My stocking had a big hole.

All my wife wants for Christmas is a five-pound box of money, gift-wrapped.

If Christmas comes, can bills be far behind?

I found something today that's cheaper than it was two weeks ago — a Christmas tree.

Christmas is the time of the year of anticipation, preparation, recreation, relation, prostration, and recuperation.

"What is your husband getting for Christmas?"
"Bald and fat."

"Why does Santa Claus have a garden?"
"He likes to hoe hoe hoe."

"Let's exchange presents at Christmas."
"Sure, I always exchange yours."

"Why don't you buy some Christmas seals?"
"I wouldn't know what to feed them."

"Is your daddy home?"
"No, sir. He hasn't been home since mother caught Santa Claus kissing the maid."

"And what did you find in your stockings on Christmas morning?"
"As usual, a big hole."

Church

My friend is so Catholic he can't get fire insurance — too many candles in his house.

Now they want to split Massachusetts in half — High Mass and Low Mass.

Churches, where souls are lifted, are empty. But beauty parlors where faces are lifted, are packed.

A preacher is a man who can keep women quiet for an hour.

It isn't true that gamblers aren't religious. You ought to hear them praying for a winner.

She sang in church last week and 200 people changed their religion.

I told him that I worship my figure and he tried to embrace my religion.

"The church choir will now sing: 'I heard the bills on Christmas day.'"

The Circus

When I was three I ran away with the circus, but the police made me bring it back.

This show is full of surprises. I just wish it was full of talent.

They got this act for many reasons. He's famous, he's handsome and he works cheap.

He gets shot from a cannon. He gets three cents a mile and traveling expenses.

"I used to be with the circus."
"What cage were you in?"

"Ma, may I go to the circus this afternoon?"
"Why do you want to go to the circus when your uncle is around?"

Clocks

What is a clock?

. . . A non-alcoholic eye opener.

. . . A device that enables men to rise in the world.

. . . Something that gets the most abuse when it does its duty.

. . . Something that has the trouble of going off while you're asleep.

. . . Something that scares the daylight out of you.

. . . A small mechanical device to wake up people who have no children.

Every time I ask what time it is I get a different answer.

"Don't throw the clock at father, mother. It's only a waste of time!"

The best part of the day is over when the alarm clock rings in the morning.

When the clock strikes 13, it's time to get it fixed.

He kept 100 clocks around the house since he heard that time is valuable.

Take a lesson from the clock: it passes the time by keeping its hands busy.

There is a new alarm clock for actors. It doesn't ring — it applauds.

One good thing about being a clock-watcher is that you are at least informed all the time of what time it is.

"Why did you throw out your alarm clock?"
"It always went off when I was asleep."

"I'd like to buy an appropriate gift. Something timely and striking."
"How about an alarm clock?"

"Why are you late for work?"
"There are eight people in our family, and the alarm was set for seven."

"Did you ever run for office?"
"Yes. I did yesterday morning when my alarm clock failed to go off."

Clothing

It isn't the cost of a strapless gown — it's the upkeep.

Every time she wears a red dress she looks like a bow-legged fire engine.

Her dress looked pretty good considering the shape it was on.

Some women show a lot of style and some styles show a lot of women.

A dress that makes one girl slim often makes others look 'round.

Her dress looked like a million dollars. All wrinkled and green.

Every year women pay more and more for less and less clothes.

She is a window dresser. Never pulls her shades down.

If a man can't see why a girl wears a strapless gown, she shouldn't.

The bride wore a beautiful gownless evening-strap.

He only rides the subway to have his clothes pressed.

"That's a nice suit you are wearing. I wonder if the style will ever come back."

Today women dress to show everything but their age.

She dresses to kill and cooks the same way.

Clothes don't make a man, but they can break a husband.

I got her something for her winter coat — mothballs.

When a woman shows up in slacks, she certainly does.

I have a suit for every day in the year — and this is it.

She always wears a dress with a square neck — to go with her head.

This suit is guaranteed not to shrink — unless it gets wet.

She looks like she dressed in front of an airplane propeller.

She has all her clothes pressed. She is on the list of the ten best-pressed girls.

I'm keeping my coat buttoned up to hide the shirt I'm not wearing.

She has absolutely nothing to wear and ten closets to keep it in.

The necklines on some of the modern dresses are really down to see level.

My raincoat has a waterproof label; the label is waterproof, but not the coat.

"Do you remember that backless, frontless, bottomless, topless evening gown I bought? I just found out it's a belt."

She bought a backless dress that was supposed to catch men. All she ever caught was a cold.

I always wear suspenders and a belt. Why be half safe?

She has worn that dress so often, it's been in style five times.

She just bought a reversible coat. What she really needs is a reversible face.

You can't judge her by her clothes — she doesn't have enough evidence.

She looks like she was poured into her dress and forgot to say when.

A smart husband hides his money in clothes that need mending.

She wears the kind of dress that starts late and ends early.

"I want to buy a mink coat."
"Something for your wife or something expensive?"

"Does your wife pick your clothes?"
"No, just the pockets."

"That suit fits you like a bandage."
"Yes, I bought it by accident."

"I want this dress in the window."
"It is in the window."

"Darling, I haven't a single decent dress."
"You wouldn't wear it if you had one."

"How come you're only wearing one glove. Did you lose one?
"No, I found one!"

"I want to buy a dress to put on around the house."
"Yes, Madam. How large is your house?"

"This suit fits you like a glove."
"That's the trouble, it should fit like a suit."

"Does he dress like a gentleman?"
"I don't know. I never saw him dress."

"Say, could I try this dress in the window?"
"We'd rather you go to the dressing room."

"This dress is too long. Do you have anything shorter?"
"Try upstairs, the belt department."

"That's a beautiful pleated shirt you are wearing."
"Those aren't pleats. It's the way my wife irons."

"I heard you bought some of those wash-and-wear pants."
"Yes, I wash them and my wife wears them."

"That's a pretty loud suit, isn't it?"
"Yes, but I got a muffler to go with it."

"Why did you tip the checkroom girl one dollar?"
"Look at the nice coat she gave me."

"You didn't have a rag on your back when I married you!"
"No, but I've plenty now!"

"Give me dresses to match my eyes."
"Sorry, we don't sell bloodshot dresses."

"What's the big party all about?"
"I'm celebrating the tenth anniversary of my new dress!"

Coffee

In America we drink our coffee out of cups. In China they drink their tea out of doors.

Whenever I complain that my coffee is cold, my wife makes it hot for me.

Don't laugh at the coffee. You, too, may be old and weak some day.

The best way to remove coffee stains from a silk blouse is with a pair of scissors.

I have heard of weak coffee, but hers is helpless.

Her coffee was so weak, it wouldn't even stain the tablecloth.

She serves half and half coffee – half in the cup and half in the saucer.

Coffee is something your parents need in the morning before you can make any noise.

We call our baby "Coffee" because he keeps us awake all night.

If this is coffee, please bring me some tea. But if this is tea, please bring me some coffee.

Her coffee is so weak it can't even hold the sugar.

She always serves me weak coffee, even though she knows I like my coffee strong and my women weak.

I would use her sugar and cream but I wouldn't touch her coffee.

"Perk up and don't drip!" as one coffee pot said to another.

I like my coffee heavy and strong. In fact, there have been times when I've bent the spoon trying to stir the coffee.

He is the kind of a guy who makes coffee nervous.

Troubles? How about the fellow who put sleeping pills in his coffee? The coffee wouldn't let him sleep and the sleeping pill wouldn't let him stay awake.

The best way to get a good cup of coffee in the morning is to wake up your wife first.

One thing about her coffee – it's not habit-forming.

She always burns my toast so it goes better with her tasteless coffee.

Of the several ways to make a good cup of coffee, sheer accident is as good as any.

We have not yet determined if a coffee-break is for stimulation, relaxation, or just plain loafing.

"How many lumps will you have in your coffee?"
"I'll take mine smooth."

"Do you feel like a cup of coffee?"
"Of course not; do I look like one?"

"Is this coffee or tea? It tastes like turpentine."
"Well, then it must be tea. Our coffee tastes like kerosene."

"Doctor, every time I drink coffee I get a stabbing pain in my left eye."
"Take the spoon out of the cup."

"Your coffee is very weak, darling."
"That's not your coffee, it's soup!"

"Say, waiter, how come there's no coffee on the menu?"
"I wiped it off."

"Waiter, this coffee tastes like tea."
"Forgive me, sir. I must have served you the hot chocolate by mistake."

"What is it about coffee that keeps you awake?"
"The high price."

"Waiter, I ordered demi-tasse and you brought me a full cup of coffee."
"So, all right. Drink only half of it."

"Waiter, I'll have a demi-tasse."
"I'll have the same thing and a cup of coffee."

"Will you give me a dime for a cup of coffee?"
"But I don't drink coffee."

"Have you enough money for a cup of coffee?"
"Oh, I'll manage somehow, thank you."

College

I won't graduate from college this year because I didn't go.

In college I majored in Pharmacy. I always wanted to be a farmer.

A professor is one who talks in other people's sleep.

I was studying to be a bone specialist. Everybody said I had the head for it.

The only thing I passed in college was the football.

Our team played so dirty we were banned in Boston.

I didn't go to college. I slept at home.

"If I'm studying when you come back, please wake me up!"

A college girl may be poor in history, but great on dates.

Some girls in my class are filled out better than their notebooks.

I can still remember my college days — all four of them.

I know a man who is so rich, he doesn't even know his son is in college.

He's a two-letter man from college. Writes home twice a week.

The only thing he really liked at college was the campus activity.

A Co-ed College is a college where the girls go in for facts and the boys go in for figures.

Every time I go to a class reunion I find my classmates are so stout and bald they hardly recognize me.

I left Harvard College because of girl trouble. There weren't any girls there — that was the trouble.

My son in college likes ties with dots, suits with stripes and letters with checks in them.

"What is your son taking in college?"
"Oh, he's taking all I've got."

"Are you a college man?"
"No, a horse stepped on my hat!"

"How were the exam questions?"
"They were easy, but I had trouble with the answers."

"I spent three years in college taking medicine."
"Are you well now?"

"What are you going to be when you graduate?"
"An old man."

"When you were in college, what did you go in for?"
"Because it was raining."

"Did you show your thesis to the professor?"
"Oh, my. Do we have to do that?"

"But officer, I'm a college man."
"I'm sorry, but ignorance is no excuse."

"So you flunked the history exam."
"Sure, they kept asking questions about things that happened before I was born."

"Can you tell me what happened in 1776?"
"I can't even remember what happened last night."

"Say, I went to college, Stupid."
"Yes, and you came back stupid."

"How is your son doing in college?"
"He must be doing pretty well in languages. I just paid for three courses: $30 for Latin, $30 for Greek, and $200 for Scotch."

"Before we begin this final exam, are there any questions?"
"Yes, sir, what's the name of this course?"

Columbus

One thing about Columbus, he didn't miss the boat.

What's so wonderful about Columbus' discovering America? It's so big, how could he miss it?

Judging from the shape the world is in, Columbus must have had the wrong theory at that.

Columbus discovered America for only one reason: he wanted to give Europe a place to borrow money from.

All Columbus did was discover America. Look what other people have done to it.

Columbus was traveling in a circle. You have heard about Columbus Circle?

"Where did Columbus stand when he discovered America?"
"On his feet."

"What bus crossed the ocean?"
"Columbus."

"On what date did Columbus cross the ocean?"
"He didn't cross on a date. He crossed on a ship."

"What was the first bus to arrive in America?"
"Columbus."

"When was Columbus born?"
"On Columbus day."

"You don't even know that Columbus found America?"
"I didn't even know it was lost."

Comedians

Is he funny? He always gets a quiet sitting ovation.

Is he funny? He couldn't cheer up a laughing hyena.

Is he funny? He appears once and suffers from over-exposure.

He'd be the funniest man if he was as well-known as his jokes.

His jokes are not funny but his delivery is terrible.

Did you hear about the comedian who told the same jokes three nights running? He wouldn't dare tell them standing still.

Cooking

My wife is such a terrible cook that she blushes after every meal.

We have now a new cook. A gem. Chicken, turkey, roast beef, you name it, it makes no difference to her. She eats everything.

Today men don't ask their wives what's cooking. They ask: "What's thawing?"

I'm not saying my wife is a bad cook, but my doctor advised me to eat out more often.

My wife found the best way to avoid cooking odor in the kitchen. She stopped cooking.

Women today may not know how to cook, but they sure know what's cooking.

A cookbook is a book with a lot of stirring chapters.

A good cook is smart enough to give the soup a different name every day.

All some girls know about cooking is how to bring a guy to a quick burn.

American cooking is the art of taking food out of containers and putting it on the plates.

Be kind to your wife and she may help you with the dishes.

Don't taste the food while cooking it, you may lose the nerve to serve it!

"Get off that stove, mother. That's no place to ride the range!"

Home cooking is what a man misses when his wife isn't.

Home cooking is where many a man thinks his wife is.

"Honey, what's this on my plate, in case I have to describe it to the doctor?"

It's not bad manners to speak with your mouth full when you're praising your wife's cooking.

EVERY TIME I eat my wife's jello I get a lump in my throat.

EVERY TIME she serves a square meal it doesn't fit my round stomach.

EVERY TIME she tries out a new recipe from her mother I get a new prescription from my doctor.

It's veal, and the chef tried to make chicken salad, but it tasted so much like turkey we call it tuna.

"Put more water into your soup. The vegetables are too close together!"

Show me a beautiful, sexy wife who doesn't like to cook and I'll show you a couple who eat out a lot.

The cook was a good cook as cooks go, and as cooks go, she went.

The man who would rather play golf than eat should marry the woman who would rather play bridge than cook.

Too many cooks spoil the figure.

No woman lives long enough to try all the recipes she clips out of papers.

What I liked best about my mother's cooking was that it didn't cost me anything.

You can't win. His first wife could cook but wouldn't. His second wife can't cook but does.

"Say, honey, are we eating out tonight? I don't smell anything burning."

"Do you know how to cook?"
"Certainly. My mother taught me yesterday."

"Why did you become a vegetarian?"
I couldn't stand to see my wife burn a $5 steak."

"Do you know anything about foreign cooking?"
"No, it's all Greek to me."

"Do you say a prayer before you eat?"
"No, we don't have to. My mother is a good cook."

"Where is the paper plate that was under the pie?"
"Oh, I thought it was the lower crust."

"I cook and bake for you and what do I get? Nothing!"
"You're lucky. I eat your cooking and always get indigestion."

"I've been cooking for ten years."
"You ought to be done by now."

"How do you like my biscuits?"
"Very good. Did you buy them yourself?"

"How long do you cook spaghetti?"
"Oh, about ten inches."

"If you marry me, I'm going to cook and darn your socks."
"Just darn them dear."

"Doctor, once again I have an upset stomach."
"How many times did I tell you not to eat your wife's cooking?"

"Is it all right to make breakfast in my nightgown?"
"Sure, but it would be less messy in a frying pan."

Courts — Crime

She had a Supreme Court figure — no appeal.

Crime doesn't pay unless, of course, you do it well.

I wanted to tell the truth, but every time I tried, my lawyer objected.

I know a burglar who is so successful, he stopped making house calls.

Crime doesn't pay but at least you're your own boss.

Can a man be arrested for striking a match?

"This pen leaks," said the convict as the rain came through the roof.

Dad is very popular in prison. He's the lifer of the party.

The judge gave me 200 years. It's lucky I didn't get life.

He was arrested for picking his way through the crowd — a pocket at a time.

A jail is the only place where they won't raise your rent.

A jury consists of 12 people who determine which side has the best lawyer.

Usually the fellow who shouts the loudest for justice is the one who wants it in his favor.

He went to jail for something he didn't do. He didn't pay his taxes.

A prisoner is the only person who doesn't mind being interrupted in the middle of a sentence.

They put me in jail because I was making big money — about an inch too big.

"Let's hurry into the patrol wagon, mother, or we'll never get a seat!"

"Of course I didn't stop when the policeman waved at me, Your Honor. I'm not that kind of a girl."

He thought a suspended sentence was a man hanging by the rope on the gallows.

The only people who still make house calls are the burglars.

"Not guilty of bigamy. You may go home."
"Thank you, Judge. Which one?"

"Gentlemen of the jury, have you reached a verdict?"
"We have. We find the man who stole the car not guilty!"

"This is the fifth time you've appeared before me. I fine you ten dollars."
"Your Honor, don't I get a discount for being a steady customer?"

"Young man, you are accused of stealing a petticoat."
"Your Honor, it was my first slip!"

"Don't you know that crime doesn't pay?"
"I know, but the hours are good."

"Didn't the burglar wake you up?"
"No, he took things very quietly."

"Guilty or not guilty?"
"What else have you got?"

"I must charge you for murder."
"All right. What do I owe you?"

"Have you ever been cross-examined before?"
"Yes, Your Honor, I'm a married man."

"Did you ever speak before a big audience?"
"Yes, I said 'Not Guilty.'"

"I see you have appeared as a witness before. In what suit?"
"My tan gabardine."

"Do you plead guilty or not guilty?"
"How should I know, Your Honor, before I've heard the evidence?"

"Have you anything to offer to the court before sentence is passed?"
"No, Judge. I had ten dollars but my lawyer took that."

"Guilty. Ten days or twenty dollars."
"I'll take the twenty dollars, Judge!"

"Did you strike that man in the excitement?"
"No, Judge. I struck him in the stomach."

"Do you realize you are facing the electric chair?"
"I don't mind facing it, it's the sitting down in it that gets me."

"Are you guilty or not guilty?"
"That seems to me a rather personal question, Judge."

"Please tell the court why you stabbed your husband 58 times."
"I didn't know how to turn off the electric knife."

"They can't put you in jail for that!"
"Oh yeah? Where do you think I'm phoning from — the public library?"

"Order, order in the court!"
"Thank you, Judge. I'll take a ham on rye."

"But Judge, I wasn't drunk. I was only drinking."
"Oh, that's different. I'm not giving you a month in jail, only 30 days."

Cows

It was so hot the cows were giving evaporated milk.

Now I know why the cow jumped over the moon. The farmer had cold hands.

It's easy to milk a cow. Any jerk can do it.

We feed our cows money and hope they will give rich milk.

To keep milk from turning sour, keep it in the cow.

It was so cold the farmer milked for twenty minutes before he found out he was only shaking hands with himself.

How come black cows eat green grass and give white milk?

He pushed a cow over the cliff so he could see the Jersey bounce.

He fed his cow batteries so he could blow her horn.

This farmer kept his cows in the ice house — trying to make them give ice cream.

"Does a cow give milk?"
"No, you have to take it from her."

"What is cowhide chiefly used for?"
"To keep the cow together."

"When can you see cows with eight feet?"
"When two cows are side by side."

"Say, waiter, this milk is weak."
"Sorry, the cow got caught in the rain."

"Do you know how long cows should be milked?"
"The same as short ones."

"Is this milk fresh?"
"Fresh? Three hours ago it was grass."

"Why does your uncle keep his cows in the house?"
"Well, he has to keep them contented, doesn't he?"

"On the farm, did you ever listen to cowbells?"
"Don't be silly. Cows don't have bells – they have horns."

"Name five things that contain milk."
"That's easy. Ice cream, butter, cheese and two cows."

Credit Cards

Credit cards are what people use after they discover that money can't buy everything.

My wife pays her Diners Club Card with her American Express Card.

I know when Father's Day is coming. My wife borrows all my credit cards.

For her birthday she just wants a few cards – like American Express Card, Diners Club Card, . . .

A credit card is a printed I.O.U.

Today you need a credit card to pay cash!

My credit is so bad, they won't even take my cash.

My wife's charge plates and credit cards are killing me!

I'm so used to buying with credit cards that when I bought something for cash I signed all the dollar bills.

Many a man's wallet would be flatter if it weren't full of credit cards.

My wife sure gets a charge out of my credit cards.

Credit cards have made buying easier but paying harder.

Credit cards help you live within your income and beyond your means.

A credit card is what you use to buy today what you can't afford tomorrow while you're still paying for it yesterday.

Money is about the only thing that's handier than credit cards.

Eat, drink and be merry today because tomorrow they might cancel your credit card.

Using a credit card is a convenient way to spend money you wish you had.

D

Dancing

You think you've got troubles? I know a fan dancer who's ticklish!

She dances like popcorn over a hot fire.

He went to the country to see a barn dance.

"May I have the next dance, please. My foot is asleep."

Dancing is very tough for me. I've got two left feet and it's hard to find a girl with two right ones.

Every time I dance with a grass widow I get hay fever.

"Waltz a little faster, dear, they are playing a rhumba!"

He does a terrific cha cha, no matter what the band is playing.

When I dance my feet never touch the floor. You see, I wear shoes.

I like a girl who can stand on her own feet, especially when dancing.

The newest dance is called "The Talk." You don't move anything but your lips.

You don't know what fear is until you have danced the tango with a girl wearing pointed shoes.

She wanted to be a bubble dancer but her dad said; "No soap!"

A wallflower is a girl who comes home wearing the same lipstick she started out with.

She was a big success as a bubble dancer until her career blew up in her face.

A hula dancer has no future. It's such a shaky business.

A striptease dancer is a girl who has everything and shows it.

I don't mind you dancing on my feet; it's the continual jumping on and off that gets me.

Some dance floors are so crowded, you can't tell who your partner is.

A rhumba is a dance where the front of you goes along nice and smooth like a Cadillac, and the back of you makes like a jeep.

I know a fellow who when he dances he's all feet and when he stops he's all hands.

An intermission at a college dance is when everyone comes inside to rest.

The dance floor was so crowded we had to do the rhumba up and down instead of sideways.

A girl is something you look damn silly dancing without.

He took his girl to a barn dance and she gave him the old stall.

She doesn't dance well, but gosh, can she intermission!

"Dancers run in my family."
"Too bad they don't dance."

"I never danced so poorly before."
"Oh, then you have danced before?"

"Let's sit this dance out."
"I'm tired; let's dance awhile."

"Have you been dancing long?"
"Yes, since six o'clock."

"Today I danced like I never danced before."
"Oh, I see, on your own feet."

"Darling, I want to dance like this forever."
"Don't you ever want to improve?"

"Do you always dance with your eyes closed?"
"I hate to see my feet suffer."

"May I have the last dance?"
"You've just had it."

"Until I met you, life was just one big desert."
"Is that why you dance like a camel?"

"Do you like meat balls?"
"I don't think I ever attended any."

"I learned to dance in one evening."
"I thought so."

"So, your girlfriend is a toe dancer."
"And how! She dances all over my toes."

"Say, doesn't this dance make you long for another?"
"Sure, but he couldn't come tonight."

"The dance floor is very slippery tonight."
"That ain't the floor. I just had my shoes shined."

"I've got dancing in my blood."
"Well, you must have a very poor circulation. It hasn't gotten to your feet yet."

"I didn't know your wife could do the Charleston."
"She isn't doing it. The waiter spilled some hot soup down her back."

Dates

When she has a heavy date, she gets into something light.

To brighten up your boyfriend's evening, sit with him in the dark.

Many a girl is more than tickled when her boyfriend calls.

Many a girl goes out on a moonlight date and comes home in a fog.

"I'm sorry, I can't see you Sunday. I'm expecting a headache."

She stood me up more times than the Star Spangled Banner.

Girls with figures make the best dates.

I never wear gloves on dates. I feel better without them.

Whenever I ask my girl out for dinner she asks me if she could bring a date.

He went over to Picadilly for a blind date and did he pick a dilly!

"Nancy! Your instant headache is here!"

I'll either have to get a larger car or take out a smaller girl.

I took her to the new wax museum and the dummies were better looking than my date.

"How about coming up to my apartment and putting your shock-proof watch to a test?"

She's been stood up more often than a bowling pin.

She had a big date with a fine fellow but neither of them showed up.

I have to have dates with good girls. I can't afford the other kind.

I used to go out with a perfect 36 until my wife came in with a loaded 45.

He took his girl for a ride and had motor trouble. His car wouldn't stall.

A blind date is when you expect a vision and she turns out to be a sight.

Then there was the dumb girl who turned a deaf ear to a blind date.

I asked her if I could see her home so she gave me a picture of it.

"What did your blind date look like?"
"Well, she looked better over the telephone."

"You're the kind of a man a girl cannot trust."
"Haven't we met before? Your faith is familiar."

"What do you mean the dates you had with Carol were like pearls?"
"Neckless, brother, neckless."

"I said, have you been out with a worse-looking fellow than I am?"
"I heard you the first time, but I'm still thinking."

"I haven't had a single date this week."
"I know. All your dates were married!"

Death

Life is wonderful. Without it you'd be dead.

Please let me die with my boots on. I've got a hole in my socks.

He was condemned to be hanged, but he saved his life by dying in prison.

In his will he left a loudspeaker to the church – in memory of his wife.

They say people live longer. They have to. The way prices are who can afford to die?

He died a natural death – he was hit by a car.

Everyone wants to go to Heaven, but nobody wants to die.

He wants to die with his boots on so he won't hurt his toes when he kicks the bucket.

This town is so healthy, the only man who ever died was the undertaker – and he starved to death.

You can see by the paper that all people die in alphabetical order.

"Did the medicine I gave your uncle straighten him out?"
"It sure did. They buried him today."

"Say, did you see the announcement of my death in the morning paper?"
"Yes, I did. Where are you calling from?"

How did he know the exact date and hour he was going to die?"
"The judge told him."

"What's the death rate around here?"
"Same as any other place. One death per person."

"If you were to die in five minutes and had ten cents in your pocket, what would you do?"
"I would buy some lifesavers."

"Doc, I'm afraid I'm going to die!"
"Nonsense! That's the last thing you'll do!"

"What kind of men go to Heaven?"
"Dead men."

"What became of the fellow who was killed yesterday?"
"Oh, he's dead."

"What do you get when you lean a corpse against a doorbell?"
"A dead ringer."

"Why do you want to be buried at sea?"
"My wife always says she is going to walk on my grave."

"So Jones is dead. Did he leave his wife much?"
"Oh, nearly every night."

The Dentist

I see my dentist twice a year — once for each tooth.

My dentist is painless. *He* doesn't feel a thing.

I always wanted to be a dentist, but I didn't have enough pull.

A real painless dentist is one who forgets to bill you.

The only person who enjoys a toothache is a dentist.

I used to be a dentist but I had to quit. Couldn't stand the grind.

Nothing can make a fellow pay an old dentist bill like a fresh toothache.

I always prefer a woman dentist. It's the only time I get to open my mouth to a woman.

A dentist married a manicurist and they've been fighting tooth and nails ever since.

My dentist got in trouble for telling jokes. He pulled too many good ones.

My dentist has no windows in his office. That's why they call him a paneless dentist.

"I told you not to swallow. Now my last pair of pliers are gone!"

"Now be a good boy and say 'Ah' so I can get my finger out of your mouth!"

I said ten dollars was a lot of money for pulling a tooth – after all, it's only five seconds work. So he pulled it slowly.

His dentist gave him a $100 bill – I mean a bill for 100 dollars.

"You don't need to open your mouth that far, madam. I expect to stand outside while pulling your tooth."

My dentist found such a big cavity he sent me to a chiropodist.

"Why did you strike the dentist?"
"He got on my nerves."

"Doc, what's good for biting fingernails?"
"Sharp teeth!"

"How was your trip to the dentist?"
"Oh, I had a drilling time."

"Hm, I see a big cavity in your mouth."
"Of course, that's my throat, Doc."

"Did you have a good time at the dentist?"
"I was bored to tears."

"Say, doc, that wasn't the tooth I wanted pulled."
"Calm yourself. I'm coming to it!"

"When I talk people listen with their mouth open."
"Oh, you must be a dentist."

"Now behave yourself. I didn't touch your tooth yet."
"I know, Doc. But you're standing on my foot!"

"You won't have to pay me now!"
"I know, Doc. But I'm just counting my money before you give me gas."

"Is he a careful dentist?"
"Well, he filled my teeth with great pain!"

"I see you have lost two teeth since I saw you last."
"I didn't lose them, Doc. I've got them here in my pocket!"

"Did your dentist hurt you much?"
"Not this time. His charge was quite reasonable."

"What are you saving all those old magazines for?"
"I'm studying to be a dentist."

"Doctor, your signs say you're a painless dentist."
"My signs are correct. I haven't a pain in my body."

"I heard your dentist charges five dollars for a cavity."
"That's right. You pay him five dollars and you get one."

"But, doctor, $15 just for pulling a tooth. Isn't that a little much?"
"Sure, but your little boy yelled so loud he chased away the other patients."

Dictionaries

Who needs a dictionary? If you've read one you've read them all.

If you can't find it in the dictionary, the atlas, or the encyclopedia, don't be discouraged. Ask for it at the drug store.

The only place where success comes before work.

The only place where divorce comes before marriage.

I can now find words in the dictionary much faster than I used to since I discovered that the words are listed in alphabetical order.

"Where does Thursday come before Wednesday?"
"In the dictionary."

"Where can happiness always be found?"
"In the dictionary."

"Where can everyone always find money?"
"In the dictionary."

"Where can you find your last speech, word for word?"
"In the dictionary."

"I don't believe half of what I see in print."
"How about a dictionary?"

"I don't know the meaning of fear."
"Why don't you look it up in the dictionary?"

"How do you like your new job?"
"I must be doing all right. My boss just bought me another dictionary."

"Have you read Webster's Dictionary?"
"No. I'll wait until they make a movie out of it."

Diets — Dinner

If you cheat on a diet you gain in the end.

An onion a day gives your diet away.

She was on a diet so long, she disappeared.

Eat, drink, and be merry, for tomorrow ye diet!

Then she went on a champagne diet. Took off $45.

She was as sweet as sugar and twice as lumpy.

She more than kept her girlish figure. She doubled it.

He was trying to lose annoying weight but his wife didn't want a divorce.

Nothing you put in a banana split is as fattening as a spoon.

She went through a 14-day diet, but all she lost was two weeks.

If you don't worry about your diet, everything may go to pot.

Give a woman an inch — and right away the whole family is on a diet!

I've been trying to lose some ugly fat, but she keeps clinging to my arm.

Many a woman reduces and reduces, but never becomes a bargain.

My friend lost over 100 pounds in one week — his wife left him!

People who don't count their calories usually have the figure to prove it!

When dieting, the thing to remember first is to forget seconds.

Skipping is a good way to reduce — skipping lunch, skipping dinner.

It's easy to stick to a diet these days. Just eat what you can afford.

People who say they are going on a diet are just wishful shrinkers.

When a girl refuses to tell her weight, she probably weighs one hundred and plenty.

A sure-fire diet is one where you never eat while your wife is talking.

A woman never knows that she is a bad loser until she goes on a diet.

"I'm walking to reduce."
"You're on the wrong road. This one goes to Boston."

"How is your wife getting along on her reducing diet?"
"Fine. She vanished last night."

"I heard your wife is on an onion diet. Did she lose anything?"
"Yes. Five pounds and four friends."

"What shall I do? My husband says I'm too fat?"
"Go to a paint store. You can get thinner there!"

"I thought you were on a diet?"
"I am. But I've had my diet and now I'm having dinner."

"And what will you do when you are as big as your mother?"
"Diet!"

"I'm putting on too much weight. What shall I do?"
"Push yourself away from the table three times a day."

"I heard you dropped 100 pounds."
"Yes, I dropped my girl friend."

My boss wanted me for dinner but I didn't fit into his oven.

Every time I have a light lunch my wife serves me a dark dinner.

Then I ordered dinner for a party of 18. And could she eat!

The best way to avoid doing the supper dishes is to take your wife out for dinner.

My wife's TV dinners melt in your mouth. I wish she'd defrost them first.

A man who will sit on a pier all day waiting to catch a fish will complain if his wife has dinner ten minutes late.

I took my wife out for a eight-course dinner — a seven-layer cake and coffee.

I've got four invitations to have dinner out, and they are all from my wife.

I asked her what we were having for dinner. She said her family.

We eat out twice a week now. She goes out for dinner on Tuesday and I go out on Friday.

My doctor advised me to give up those intimate dinners for four unless I have three people eating with me.

Announcement: Will the party who invited us for dinner please call again — we lost the address.

A cannibal is a man who sometimes has his friends for dinner.

My wife first finds out what I want for dinner and then tries to find a restaurant that serves it.

My wife's idea of a seven-course dinner is a roll of bologna and a six-pack.

"May I sit on your right hand at dinner?"
"I may need it to eat with, but you may hold it awhile."

"Does your wife know you're bringing me home for dinner?"
"Does she? We argued about it all morning."

"I've got a surprise for you, honey. I brought a friend home for dinner."
"Who wants to eat friends?"

"Now, Mary, when you wait on the guests at dinner don't spill anything."
"Don't worry, Ma'am. I won't say a word."

"Welcome home, darling. I've got dinner almost ready. I have candles and wine on the table."
"But I don't want to eat candles and wine for dinner."

"Waiter, I'll take the dollar dinner."
"On white or rye bread?"

"I invited you to come after dinner."
"That's what I have come after."

"What else would you like for your dinner?"
"The blonde sitting over there."

"We are having mother for dinner, darling."
"Make sure she's well done."

"At a buffet dinner, should one serve boiled eggs?"
"One should serve whoever shows up."

"How many times have I told you not to be late for dinner?"
"I don't know. I thought *you* were keeping score."

Discoveries

I have discovered something that does the work of ten men: Ten women.

He discovered a sure cure for amnesia but kept forgetting what it was.

I discovered how to hammer nails without hitting my thumb. Let someone else hold the nail.

I work on nothing but important discoveries — like bananas you can put in the refrigerator.

I just discovered something that cooks, cleans, washes the dishes and scrubs the floor — it's called a wife.

He discovered a soap that leaves your wash rough and red but your hands come out whiter than new.

They laughed when I discovered a new kind of dynamite, but when I dropped it, they exploded.

Then I discovered that when I put an electric toaster in my mattress, I can pop right out of bed each morning.

Then I found out that every time I put popcorn in my pancakes they turn over by themselves.

Divorce

The chief cause of all divorces is matrimony.

Judging by the divorce rate, a lot of people who said "I do," don't.

She is a fine housekeeper. Every time she gets a divorce she keeps the house.

A divorce costs much more than a marriage, but it's worth it.

My wife is suing for divorce and she's asking for custody of the money.

She lost the marriage but she won the divorce.

They got a divorce because of religious differences. She worshipped money and he didn't have a dime.

I want a divorce because everything my wife says, does and cooks disagrees with me.

Divorce has become so common that my wife and I are staying married just to be different.

They have trouble getting a divorce because nobody wants the children.

"Doctor, I have a small, embarrassing wart."
"Divorce him."

"Why did you poison your husband?"
"We couldn't afford a divorce."

"I hear you're going to divorce your husband."
"Don't be silly. Why, I hardly know him."

"What do you want for Christmas, honey?"
"A divorce."

"I heard you bought some real estate in Reno."
"Yes, it's only to have grounds for divorce."

"Did you get rid of your old dishwasher?"
"Yes, I divorced him."

"So you want a divorce. Aren't your relations pleasant?"
"Mine are, but hers are terrible."

"I'm going to get a divorce. My wife hasn't spoken to me in six months.
"Better think it over. Wives like that are hard to get."

"Why don't you give your husband a divorce?"
"What, I have lived with him for ten years and now I should make him happy?"

"You want a divorce because your husband is careless about his appearance?"
"Yes, he hasn't showed up in two years."

"Why do you want a divorce?"
"Every time I sit on my husband's lap he starts dictating."

Doctors

The best way to get a doctor to make a housecall is to marry him.

I wonder what she meant when she told the doctor to cut it out?

When she swallowed a nickel the doctor made her cough up four dollars.

I was thinking of becoming a doctor. I have the handwriting for it.

When I told my doctor about my loss of memory he made me pay in advance.

My friend figured there were too many people in the world so he became a doctor.

Many a girl who doesn't get taken out has an appendix that does.

My wife just changed doctors. The first one had no TV in his waiting-room.

Doctors have made great medical progress in the past generation. What used to be an itch is now an allergy.

On her first visit to the doctor, she gave him a preamble of her constitution.

The doctor felt the patient's purse and admitted that there was nothing he could do.

Some doctors tell their patients the bad news man to man; others prefer to send the bill by mail.

Our party line is so busy, the quickest way to get a doctor is to put an ad in the paper.

My brother is now studying to become a doctor. Not that he likes medicine so much, but he is crazy about double-parking.

It is almost impossible to find a doctor who is poor, even though there are many poor doctors.

Most doctors pour drugs of which they know little, to cure diseases of which they know less, into human beings of which they know nothing.

A doctor is the only man who can tell a woman to take off all her clothes and then send her husband a bill for it.

Medical science says that whiskey can't cure the common cold, but neither can medical science.

Those new miracle drugs are so wonderful. Now a doctor can keep his patient alive long enough to pay his bill.

What's the use of consulting the doctor about a cold if it gives you heart disease when you get the bill.

They say an apple a day keeps the doctor away. I say: an onion a day will keep everybody away.

"And why shouldn't I cough more easily, Doctor? I was practicing all night?"

"I can't pay your bill, Doctor. I slowed down as you told me and I lost my job!"

"Oh, Doctor, I thought you were never coming and that I'd have to die without your help!"

"It's nice of you, Doctor, to send my wife away for a rest. Heaven knows I need it!"

I sacrificed everything so that my son could become a doctor, and now he tells me I have to stop smoking!

"Yes, Doctor, I'll give up wine, women and song. I'm tapering off with beer, one girl and a little humming."

He is a fine baby doctor and he'll be even better when he grows up.

"Doc, my wife's got laryngitis. What can she take that'll clear it up in a month or two?"

"Doc, I'm slowly going nuts over women. Is there anything to speed it up?"

They now have a doctor doll: you wind it up and it operates on batteries.

This doctor turned kidnaper, but failed because nobody could read the ransom notes.

When I told my doctor I only drink to calm my nerves he said that nobody's nerves are that noisy.

"You should consult my doctor. You will never live to regret it!"

I went to a doctor for a complete checkup and the first thing he did while I undressed was to examine my wallet.

"Well Mr. Smith, let me put it this way. The softness of your muscles is exceeded by the hardness of your arteries."

When I complained to my doctor about insomnia he sent me home to sleep it off.

"Oh, I finally found a perfect doctor. Every time I go to him, he finds something wrong with me."

"Yes, the doctor will consider a house call. What time can you be at his house?"

"Now then, you have to forget wine, women and song. Just have tea and television."

A doctor is the only man who hasn't a guaranteed cure for a cold.

One doctor to another: "I usually take two aspirin every four patients."

"First let me start with your medical history. Do you pay your doctor bills promptly?"

If it takes an apple a day to keep the doctor away, what does it take to get rid of the nurse?

"I know you're very sick and running a high fever, and you're only a few blocks from here. But mother, you know I make no house calls!"

He wants to be a doctor, only to be able to park in a Hospital Zone.

"Quick, doctor, tell me, is it a boy?"
"Well, the one in the middle is!"

"Doc, I have a pain in my left foot."
"Try walking with the other."

"Does your husband exercise?"
"Yes, doctor, last week he was out four nights running."

"How did you get that splinter in your finger?"
"I scratched my head, Doctor."

"Doc, I need something to stimulate me, to put me in fighting trim."
"You'll find all that in your bill."

"Young man, you owe your fine recovery to your wife's tender care."
"Thank you doctor. I will make out the check to my wife."

"I heard the tree surgeon had an accident."
"Yes, he fell out of his patient."

"The test shows that you're a kleptomanic."
"What can I take for it, Doctor?"

"Doctor, I often feel like killing myself. What shall I do?"
"Leave it to me."

"Hello, Doctor, I can't sleep. Can you do anything for me?"
"Hold onto the phone. I'll sing you a lullaby."

"Why are you jumping up and down like that?"
"The doctor just gave me a medicine and he forgot to shake the bottle."

"Doctor, your wife wants you to call her at home."
"Tell her I don't make any house calls."

"Doc, there's something wrong with my stomach."
"Keep your coat buttoned and no one will notice it."

"Am I getting better, Doctor?"
"I don't know. Let me feel your purse."

"I don't feel so good, Doctor."
"Let me give you a complete check-up. You will never live to regret it."

"Nobody lives forever!"
"Mind if I try, Doctor?"

"Have you ever had a murmur?"
"Sure, Doc, and a purpur too."

"Well, Doc. How do I stand?"
"I don't know. It's a miracle."

"I'm the doctor's nurse."
"Oh, is the doctor sick?"

"Did the doctor treat you yesterday?"
"No, he charged me ten dollars."

"Did someone take your pulse?"
"No, Doc. I still have it."

"So your doctor saved your life."
"Yes, I called and he didn't come."

"I'm having trouble breathing, Doc."
"Well, I can stop that."

"I will examine you for ten dollars."
"Go ahead, Doc. If you find it you can have it."

"Doctor, do you think I will live?"
"Yes, but I don't advise it."

"Are you taking your medicine regulary?"
"No, Doc. I tasted it and decided to keep on coughing."

"Doctor, what am I really allergic to?"
"Paying my bills."

"How do you want your medicine today?"
"With a fork."

"How long can a man live without a brain, Doc?"
"I don't know. How old are you?"

"I heard your doctor has a new shock treatment?"
"Sure, he sends you the bill in advance."

"Doctor, every bone in my body hurts."
"Be glad you're not a herring."

Dogs

I once bought a lap dog but I had to get rid of him. Every time I sat on his lap he bit me.

One dog said to another: "What happened to me shouldn't happen to a man."

My friend has a fine watch dog. At any suspicious noise he wakes the dog and the dog begins to bark.

There are stories that dogs can talk. It's untrue. If any dog tells you he can talk, he's lying.

A dog is known as a man's best friend, because it gives no advice, never tries to borrow money and has no in-laws.

We have a fine watch dog. Last week he watched the garage burn down, then he watched somebody steal our lawn mower, then he watched . . .

If a man bites a dog, he's probably eating a frankfurter.

He made his dog sit in the sun. Wanted to get a hot dog.

I call my dog "Photographer" because he is always snapping people.

A dog is the only friend you can buy for money.

I was the teacher's pet. She couldn't afford a dog.

He's a very smart dog. In only two weeks he taught me how to give a paw.

Some dogs are pointers; mine is a nudger. He's too polite to point.

My dog works for the fire department. He helps locate hydrants.

My dog is a lousy bloodhound. I cut my hand once and he fainted.

My dog is a bird dog, but I never heard him sing.

We bought a dachshund so that all the children could pet him at the same time.

I've hated dogs ever since I went to a masquerade ball as a lamp post.

He is a doberman pincher. All day he goes around pinching dobermans.

My dog is afraid of burglars. I had to put an alarm system in his dog house.

A dog has so many friends because he wags his tail instead of his tongue.

I have to get my dog a present or he'll bite my husband again.

I got this dog for my wife. I wish I could make a trade like that every day.

Perhaps it's only a coincidence, but man's best friend can't talk.

A dachshund is a dog who wags his tail by remote control.

No, Henry, a dogma is not a mama dog!

Dogs in Siberia are the fastest in the world because the trees are so far apart.

Did you hear about the army dog that wanted to be transferred to a new post?

Did you hear about the dog that visited a flea circus and stole the show?

A barking dog never bites — while barking.

A dog is cheaper than a wife. The license costs less and he already has a fur coat.

"Why is your dog staring at me like that?"
"Probably because you're eating from his dish."

"Do you know that your dog barked all night?"
"Yes, but don't worry. He sleeps all day."

"I like this dog but his legs are too short."
"Too short? They reach the floor, don't they?"

"Look here, don't you know my office hours are from 8 to 10?"
"Yes, doctor, but the dog that bit me didn't."

"You play chess with your dog? He must be very smart."
"Oh no, he isn't. I beat him most of the time."

"Say, your puppy just bit me in the ankle."
"Well, you don't expect a little dog to bite you on the neck, do you?"

"You have seen people riding horses, but have you ever seen people ride dogs?"
"I did. 50 on a Greyhound."

"I want you to keep that dog out of the house. It's full of fleas."
"Fido! Don't go in the house. It's full of fleas!"

"I know a dog worth $10,000."
"How could a dog save so much?"

Dreaming

To make your dream come true, you have to stay awake!

If I ever find the girl of my dreams, what will I do with my wife?

"Say, you can't be real. May I pinch you to see if I'm dreaming?"

Last night I got a double rest. I dreamed I was sleeping.

No wife minds her husband being a dreamer as long as he isn't a snorer.

That's the kind of girl I dream about. You should see the one I wake up with.

Dreaming is the only time you meet a better class of people.

When some girls dream of rice it's a wedding. When an old maid dreams of rice, it's pudding.

A dreamer is a person who goes through life having a wonderful time spending money he hasn't got.

"If I dream again that you kissed another woman, so help me, I'll divorce you!"

"I dreamed that I died and went to Heaven."
"What woke you up? The heat?"

"I dreamed that I had a tough job."
"Yes, you do look tired."

"I dreamed you bought me a fur coat."
"In your next dream, wear it in good health, honey."

"I dreamed last night that I proposed to the best girl in the world."
"And what did I answer?"

"I'd like to make your dreams come true."
"I'll slap your face if you try."

"What did you dream last night?"
"I don't know. I slept through most of it."

"Why are you wearing your glasses in bed?"
"I wanna get a better look at the girls I dreamed about last night."

Drinks — Drinking

Did you hear about the fellow who . . .

. . . drank eight cokes and burped 7-up?

. . . spilled some beer on the stove. Now he has foam on the range?

. . . put his wine on the top of the house to keep up his spirits?

. . . saved all his money he would have spent on beer and spent it on beer?

. . . took a ladder to the party because he heard the drinks were on the house?

She only drinks to forget she drinks.

I never drink unless I'm alone or with somebody.

Liquor may be slow poison, but who's in a hurry?

If you drink to forget, forget it!

He's not a steady drinker. His hands shake too much.

She drinks so much alcohol I'm afraid to let her smoke.

Be aware of those eye openers. Too many and you can't see!

I knew I was drunk. I felt sophisticated and couldn't pronounce it!

Nothing makes a woman look better than three cocktails inside a man.

My wife sent me down for a pint. I brought her some ice cream.

My wife can cook like her mother and drink like her father.

I can tell when my girl drinks. Her face starts getting blurred.

The only thing he can fix around the house are Manhattans and Martinis.

He drank so much beer that when he ate a pretzel you could hear it splash.

He is such a heavy drinker he didn't know the water was cut off for two months.

The best way to hold liquor is in a glass.

They make such a dry martini you have to use a spoon.

He has leaned on so many bars his clothes have padded elbows.

I'm watching my drinking. I only visit bars that have mirrors.

Nobody cares how bad your English is as long as your Scotch is good.

"Junior, mother's not going to give you any more martinis if all you do is eat the olives."

The man who enters a bar very optimistically often comes out very misty optically.

"This liquor is 20 years old."
"Don't let it live another minute."

"Will you stop drinking for me?"
"What makes you think I was drinking for you?"

"Would you like a lemon with your tea?"
"No, I prefer to be alone."

"How about a little gin rummy?"
"No thanks. I never touch the stuff."

"Darling, the whole world revolves around you."
"Well, I told you not to take that last drink."

"I'm so thirsty my tongue is hanging out."
"Gee! I thought it was your tie!"

"I heard your uncle lost his glasses."
"Yes, now he has to drink from the bottle."

"Did you get drunk at the party last night?"
"No, someone beat me to the punch."

"I heard you don't drink anymore tea?"
"No, the last time the teabag got stuck in my throat."

"What would you like to drink? Scotch? Rye? Gin? Ale?"
"Yes."

"Do you ever feel your liquor?"
"Of course not. Why should I get my fingers wet?"

"Where can one get a drink, day or night?"
"In Sing Sing — that place is full of bars."

"They say whiskey and gasoline don't mix."
"They do but it tastes lousy."

"Is there any lunch in the ice box?"
"Not a drop."

Drugstores

"And this tonic will not only cure any ailment, but when you read the wrapper on the bottle, you'll have more new diseases."

What silly advertising! They say: Take Bromo-Seltzer for a headache. Who wants a headache?

In these days of drug store luncheonettes, a registered druggist certainly has to know his onions.

A pharmacist is a man in a white coat who stands behind a soda fountain selling two-dollar watches.

They now have a pill that's half aspirin and half glue. It's for people who get splitting headaches.

They just found a new drug that cures penicillin.

Then there is the hungry man who starved to death trying to get the cellophane wrapper off a drugstore sandwich.

The fellow who figured out how to get 35,000 units of vitamins in one tiny capsule must have been a bus driver.

This new wonder drug is so powerful, you have to be in perfect health to take it.

"Say, doc, have you anything good for mosquito bites on top of poison ivy over a sunburn?"

"Are you trying to tell me you don't sell sleds. What kind of a drugstore is this?"

"Could I have a penny's worth of flea powder? Don't wrap it — just blow it down my back!"

This laxative is so strong, when you buy it the druggist always gives you your change in dimes.

These new miracle drugs sound so good, I'm sorry I'm in perfect health.

He tiptoed into the drugstore because he didn't want to wake the sleeping pills.

A miracle drug is any drug you can get the kids to take without any screaming.

There was an educated drugstore soda-jerk who called himself a Fizzician.

A wonder drug is a medicine that makes you wonder whether you can afford it.

"Say, let me have some more of those sleeping pills you made up for my wife. She woke up again."

"I want some rat poison."
"Should I wrap it up or do you want to eat it right here?"

"What smells most in a drugstore?"
"The nose."

"Doctor, you gave my wife arsenic instead of sleeping powder!"
"That's O.K. You only owe me another ten cents."

"You should cut out those pills. They could be habit forming."
"Nonsense. I've been taking them for 12 years."

"I want a bottle of Iodine."
"Sorry, but this is a drugstore. How about a cheese sandwich?"

"He is a great druggist, isn't he?"
"He is, but he makes the chicken salad too salty."

"Are you sure one bottle of this will cure a cold?"
"It must. Nobody ever came back for a second."

E

Ears

My ear is ringing. Pardon me while I answer it.

My early struggle started when mother tried to wash my ears.

My child has sensitive ears. He screams every time I pull them.

Her ears are so big she looks like a taxicab with both doors open.

She has ears like a shovel – always picking up dirt.

All day long I had a ringing in my ears. Then I picked up the phone and it stopped.

She sure has big ears! From the front she looks like a loving cup.

The only time she washes her ears is when she eats watermelon.

I don't know. That must be a face – it has ears on it.

He is a big ear doctor. He only looks at big ears.

A rumor is something that goes in one ear and in another.

"Doctor, there's something wrong with my finger. Every time I put it in my ear, I can't hear!"

"Don't holler in my ear."
"Excuse me, I thought it was a microphone."

"I play piano by ear."
"Doesn't it interfere with your earrings?"

"Why doesn't the corn like the farmer?"
"Because he picks his ears."

"I know a girl who plays piano by ear."
"I know an old man who fiddles with his whiskers."

"Everything she says goes in one ear and out the other."
"Yes, there is nothing to block traffic."

"Last night I heard a bad noise in my ears."
"Where else did you expect to hear noise?"

"Were the peppers too hot, darling?"
"No, dear, Smoke always comes out of my ears when I eat."

"It seems that everything I say to you goes in one ear and out the other."
"Well, I guess that's why I've got two ears."

Easter

I had to wear a yellow-checkered jacket to match my wife's Easter outfit.

Have you noticed how many women mistake Easter for Decoration Day?

Today is Easter Sunday and my girl didn't come home yet from the office Christmas Party.

I didn't bother to hide any Easter eggs this year. The children didn't find the ones I hid last year.

Eggs

Did you ever notice that a hard-boiled egg is yellow inside?

In this place they always serve scrambled eggs so you never know how many you are getting.

Remember, an egg is a whole day's work for a chicken.

My wife can only boil eggs for five seconds. She claims if she holds them longer in the boiling water she burns her hand.

Every morning my wife makes scrambled eggs. She puts one egg on the table and we both scramble for it.

She is so dumb, she tried to open an egg with a can opener.

She has been in more hot water than a boiled egg.

She boiled an egg for ten minutes and it never got soft.

She makes eggnog with hard-boiled eggs.

Once she even tried to scramble a hard-boiled egg.

A hard-boiled egg is hard to beat.

When you want to make some omelettes, make sure you have some eggs.

An egg is something that is never beaten when it is bad.

She serves the softest hard-boiled egg you have ever seen.

"Waiter, we want a chicken. The younger the better."
"How about some soft-boiled eggs?"

"Our hen can lay an egg four inches long. Can you beat that?"
"Yes, with an egg beater."

"What's wrong with these eggs, waiter?"
"I don't know. I only laid the table."

"Those eggs just came from the country."
"What country?"

"Sir, on your order for an egg sandwich, will you take it out or eat it here?"
"Both."

"I heard egg shampoo is good for your hair."
"Yes, but how are you gonna get a chicken to lay an egg on your head?"

Electricity

He is crazy about electricity. Should we call him a electric fan?

He must use an electric shaver. He has a face only a motor could love.

He who is always blowing a fuse is usually in the dark.

He bought her an electric typewriter. Now if he only could find a chair to match....

He uses an electric toothbrush. Now he has to see an electrician twice a year.

I gave my electrician some shorts for Christmas.

"Did you ever touch a live wire?"
"No, but I heard it is a shocking experience."

"I heard your boyfriend is an electrician."
"Yes, he alternates between me and the girl next door."

"I heard your brother is a conductor. Railroad or musical?"
"Electrical. He was hit by lightning."

Elephants

Once there was an elephant who went away to forget.

Do I have a good memory? I even remind elephants.

You look like an elephant who's trying to forget.

She's got a memory like an elephant and a shape to match.

Elephants are modest. They always bathe with their trunks.

Be thankful you are not an elephant with sinus trouble.

They say an elephant never forgets. What has he got to remember?

I can lift an elephant with one hand. But where can you find an elephant with one hand?

One reason why elephants drink so much water is that no one offers them anything else.

Elephants are found in Africa, although they're so big they hardly ever get lost.

Right away I knew it was an elephant. I could smell the peanuts on his breath.

When big elephants have big trunks do little elephants have suitcases?

"Mom, where do elephants come from — and don't give me the gag about the stork again."

"Do you allow elephants on this train?"
"Yes, but you have to check their trunks."

"I want to do something big and something clean."
"Then wash an elephant."

"Why do you call your Volkswagen 'Elephant'?"
"Because it has the trunk in front."

"How much did the psychiatrist charge the elephant?
"$35 for the visit and $300 for the couch."

Embarrassments

A stitch in time saves embarrassing exposure.

A girl used to blush when embarrassed. Now she's embarrassed when she blushes.

Nothing is so embarrassing as watching your boss do something you told him couldn't be done.

She was so embarrassed. She tripped over the roses in the rug.

Embarrassment of embarrassments: two eyes meeting through a keyhole.

I am financially embarrassed. I'm eight dollars short of having 20 cents.

An embarrassing moment is spitting out of a car window when it's not open.

She was so embarrassed. She opened the refrigerator and saw a Russian dressing.

I won't say what he did, but even my shock-proof watch was embarrassed.

Yesterday I called my wife "Mary," which is very embarrassing, because her name is Sue!

Enemies

Speak well of your enemies. Remember — you made them!

The best way to avoid enemies is to outlive them.

You can even spell enemies in three letters: F-O-E.

He hasn't an enemy in the world, but all his friends hate him.

Alice never lets anyone but her close friends kiss her. That's why she doesn't seem to have any enemies.

If you can't love your enemies, compromise — forget them.

England

He reminds me of London — always in a fog.

Take a perfect day, add six hours of rain and fog and you have instant London.

She may be English, but the look in her eyes is international.

"I lost 20 pounds while I was in England."
"How much is that in American money?"

"Say, in England do you also have a blood bank?"
"No, but we have a liver-pool."

"Did you see some ruins while you were in England?"
"Sure I did. And one of them wanted to marry me."

Eskimos

When Eskimos meet they rub noses. Americans rub fenders.

It took him six months to sing "Night and Day." He was an Eskimo.

It gets so cold in Alaska, the Eskimos go to Siberia for the winter.

"Now remember, children, I want you to play on this side of the North Pole."

A snowbank is not a place where Eskimos keep their money.

Some Eskimos are poor skiers and some skiers are poor Eskimos.

"It says here that the Eskimos eat whale meat and blubber."
"You'd blubber too if you had to eat whale meat."

"What do you know about Eskimos?"
"I eat their pies."

Etiquette

Some people have tact and others tell the truth.

I never stir my coffee with my right hand. I use a spoon.

The well-bred man steps on his cigarette so it won't burn the rug.

No man is justified for spitting in another man's face, unless his mustache is on fire.

It is such bad manners to dip bread in the gravy, but it is such good taste.

He is so polite he always takes off his hat when he mentions his own name.

Every day I give my seat on the bus to somebody. I walk to work.

You know, all these years I've been eating with the wrong fingers.

He is so polite, he wouldn't open an oyster without knocking on the shell first.

She is so modest, she pulls down the shade to change her mind.

She is so modest, she blindfolds herself while taking a bath.

In polite society, whispering is not aloud.

Social tact is making your company feel at home, even though you wish they were.

She is so dignified, every time she throws a cup at her husband she takes the spoon out first.

He is really very polite. He always takes his shoes off before putting his feet on the table.

It may be bad etiquette for a husband to walk between his wife and the shop windows, but it is sure smart.

Eyes

When he took his eye examination, the doctor called off the letters on the chart and he answered true or false.

The man who knows everything under the sun usually has shadows under his eyes.

She had such bad eyes, she had to wear contact lenses to see her glasses.

"Say, Doctor, about those eyedrops, do I take them before or after meals?"

I always wear sunglasses on rainy days. They protect my eyes from umbrellas.

I know carrots are good for the eyes, but I nearly go blind every time I stick them in.

My wife gave me a present and my eyes popped out — a shirt, size 12.

"Let's wash the windows, mother. The neighbors are straining their eyes!"

I lost my glasses and can't look for them until I find them.

My eyes were never good and I have a wife to prove it.

She had something that'd knock your eyes out: a husband.

I see good in all things with one exception. I can't see good in the dark.

I had bad eyesight until I was eight. Then I got a haircut.

Many people have social circles under their eyes.

The only time some girls draw a line is when they use an eyebrow pencil.

Because a girl closes her eyes when she is being kissed is no sign she is not wide awake.

If you give up wearing eyeglasses, you look better but you don't see as well.

A green light in a woman's eye is no signal for a man to go ahead.

If brown eyes are evidence of weak will, then black eyes are evidence of a strong won't!

My girl is so wealthy the rings under her eyes have diamonds in them.

"How did you get that black eye?"
"I was hit by a guided muscle."

"Why did you wake me up? It's still dark."
"Well, open your eyes!"

"Where'd you get those big eyes?"
"They came with the face."

"How did you get that black eye?"
"Her husband heard me cough in the closet."

"Tell me, who wrote 'Oh, say, can you see'?"
"An eye doctor."

"Doctor, when I drive on sunny days I get the sun in my eyes. What should I do?"
"Drive only on cloudy days."

"Have your eyes ever been checked?"
"No, Doctor, they've always been brown."

"Doc, every time I drink hot tea I get a sharp pain in my left eye."
"Take the spoon out of your cup."

"My grandfather lived to be 95 and never used glasses."
"Lots of people drink from the bottle."

"I've never seen such dreamy eyes like yours."
"You've never stayed so late before."

"I can see good in all things."
"Can you see good in a fog?"

"Your eyes intoxicate me."
"It must be the eyeballs."

"They tell me you kiss with your eyes open."
"Yes, I always look before I lip."

"Are you married?"
"No, I got this black eye from a friend."

"Your last grapefruit was terrible."
"Wait till you get an eyeful of this one!"

F

Faces

Be it ever so homely, there's no face like hers.

There is only one trouble with her face. It shows.

The only time her face gets washed is when she cries.

They couldn't lift her face so they lowered her body.

Some girls have dishpan hands. She has a dishpan face.

There's beauty in her face if you can read between the lines.

"I never forget a face, but in your case I'll make an exception."

"The last time I saw a face like yours was on an Iodine bottle."

If her face is her fortune, she'll never have to pay income tax.

There is only one thing wrong with her face. It sticks out of her dress.

In the morning, without make-up, her face looks like the preview of a horror show.

The sooner I never see her face again, the better it will be for both of us when we meet.

The only way she can get some color in her face is to stick her tongue out.

She had such a pretty chin, she added two more.

Whether you're handsome or ugly, it's always nice to have a face.

"Did you use gunpowder on your face? It looks shot!"

"Is that your face or did you forget to wash this morning?"

She cooks the kind of meals that put color in your face — Purple!

"Is that your real face or are you still wearing the gas mask?"

She always keeps her mirrors clean. Who wants to see dusty wrinkles?

She bought a green pool table to match her face.

I never forget a face, and in your case I'll remember both of them.

A girl's face may be her fortune, but the other parts draw interests.

I never remember a name but I always forget a face.

You can't save face if you lose your head.

If you spit against the wind you get it in the face.

A face is something a girl wears off as the evening wears on.

He is ready for television. Look at his face — it's already blurred.

It is better for a woman to be two-faced than double-chinned.

"Are you familiar with Grace Smith?"
"I tried it once and she slapped my face."

"Her face looks like a million, you say?"
"Yes, all green and wrinkled."

"Do you think I should let my hair grow?"
"Yes, right over your face."

"Do you want to buy a hand mirror?"
"No, I want one I can see my face in."

"Sonny, how did you get your hands so dirty?"
"Washing my face."

"Say, how did you get all those freckles?"
"I fell asleep next to a screen door."

"I heard your girl has a complexion like a peach."
"Yes, yellow and fuzzy."

"I'll have you know that I have a face of an 18-year old child."
"Give it back. You're getting it all wrinkled."

"I entered the face-making contest."
"You did? Who won second prize?"

Families

"Don't yell at me, Mac, I'm not your mother!"

They had four sons. The first was a banker, the second was also in jail. The third was a college graduate and the fourth couldn't get a job either.

A lot of women don't care who wears the pants in the family, as long as there is money in the pockets.

She took after her mother who took after her father who took after the maid.

Did you hear about the wife who shot her husband with a bow and arrow because she didn't want to wake the children?

"You haven't nagged me all evening, honey. Is there someone else?"

Any of your friends can become an enemy, but a relative is one from the start.

They are a perfect pair. She's a hypochondriac and he's a pill.

We like to do the same things. When my wife waxes the floor I take a bottle and polish it off.

They belong to the horsey set. He is a work horse and she's a clothes horse.

"I thought you were yourself, but now that you have come closer, I see that you are your brother."

He has ordinary parents. His mama was a bearded lady and so was his papa.

Success is relative. The more success, the more relatives.

He asked his mother to sit on the front step. He always wanted to have a step mother.

For a mother the son always shines.

He shot both his parents so he could go to the orphan's picnic.

If a man doesn't like his aunt is he anti-aunty?

"Do you have a family tree?"
"We don't even have a flowerpot."

"My father can beat your father."
"Big deal. So can my mother!"

"Have you got any brothers?"
"No, but my sister does."

"I'm going back to my mother."
"That's better than her coming here."

"So you want to become my son-in-law?"
"Not exactly. I just want to marry your daughter."

"One more word and I go back to mother!"
"Taxi!"

"Mommy, am I descended from a monkey?"
"I really don't know. I've never met your father's people."

"I understand your wife came from a fine old family."
"Came is hardly the word. She brought it with her!"

"I understand his salary goes into five figures."
"Yes, his wife and four children."

"My father was a Pole."
"North or South?"

"When did your parents marry?"
"A long time before I was born."

"Has there been any insanity in your family?"
"Yes, doctor. My husband thinks he's the boss."

"But give me one good reason why you can't marry me."
"I'll give you four. My wife and three children."

"I wouldn't even cash a check for my own brother."
"Well, I guess you know your family best."

Farming

He is a gentleman farmer. Owns two station wagons and a flower pot.

He bought a farm five miles long and two inches wide. Plans to raise spaghetti.

The hardest thing to learn about farming is getting up at five a.m.

I worked on a tomato farm. It was the first time I ever picked up a tomato without whistling first.

An agriculturist is a farmer with a station wagon.

His farm is so small that cows only give condensed milk.

A gentleman farmer is one who tips his hat every time he passes a tomato.

I know a farmer who packed up and moved to the city when he heard the country was at war.

A farm is a hunk of land on which, if you get up early enough mornings and work late enough nights, you'll make a fortune — if you strike oil.

It's pretty hard on a farm. You go to sleep with the chickens, get up with the roosters, work like a horse, eat like a pig, and they treat you like a dog.

There's something about farm life that gets you — especially if the wind is blowing in the wrong direction.

Then I planted cabbages and razor blades and got a fine crop of cole slaw.

Fathers

My father told me everything about the birds and the bees. He doesn't know anything about girls!

He tried to put his father into the icebox so he could have a frozen pop.

Father's Day is the day to remember the forgotten man.

Father's Day is a holiday when your son lets you wear your new necktie first.

Father's Day always worries me. I'm afraid I'll get something I can't afford.

Last Father's Day my son gave me something I've always wanted — the keys to my car.

Do you know what I got for Father's Day? The bill for Mother's Day!

I'm getting my father something he never had before — a job!

Father's Day is the day when father goes broke giving his family money so they can surprise him with gifts he doesn't need.

Fighting

The best way to fight a woman is with a hat. Grab it and run!

My grandfather was an old Indian fighter. My grandma was an old Indian.

We've been married ten years and we've had only one quarrel. It started on our wedding day and hasn't ended yet!

She is a lady bullfighter. Fights only lady bulls.

We're really inseparable. In fact, it takes six people to pull us apart.

"All right, men, what's the fight about?"
"He called me a dirty number, warden!"

"Why did you hit your wife with a chair?"
"I couldn't lift the table."

"You must not fight. You should love your enemy."
"But he's not my enemy. He's my brother!"

Fire

She told him to go to blazes so he joined the Fire Department.

When an old flame corners a fellow, he starts looking for a fire escape.

An efficiency expert put unbreakable glass in all the fire alarms.

The best way to make a fire by rubbing two sticks together is to make sure one of them is a match.

There was a fireman who had to resign because his wife claimed he was concentrating too much on old flames.

We have a new fire department now. If your house catches fire, you can have the ashes rare, medium or well-done.

When his house caught fire he started to dig a well.

He thinks a fire engine is an engine that creates fires.

He thinks a fireplace is a place where you get fired.

He thinks a fire commissioner gets a commission on every fire.

He thinks a fire sale is a place to buy some fires.

He thinks a fire house is a place where they keep fire.

When his house caught fire, he turned on all the faucets.

He walked into the livingroom and saw his son sitting in front of a blazing fire. That disturbed him very much since he doesn't have a fireplace.

Fish

The only opportunity a fish has to take a shower is to jump up when it rains.

You think you have trouble? My goldfish gets seasick!

If you wish to eat lobster, you have a Fish Dish Wish.

The best way to keep fish from smelling is to cut off their noses.

The best way to communicate with a fish is by dropping him a line.

Fish is supposed to be brain food, and yet people eat it on Friday and then do the silliest things over the weekend.

A fish should swim four times: in water, in sauce, in wine and in the stomach.

"What is quicker than a fish?"
"Someone who can catch it."

"Why are fish smart?"
"Because they travel in schools."

"Where would you go to see a man-eating fish?"
"A seafood restaurant."

"What part of the fish weighs the most?"
"The scales."

"What's the best way to catch a fish?"
"Have someone throw it at you."

"Which animal travels the greatest distance?"
"The goldfish. It travels around the globe."

"You claim that fish are musical?"
"Certainly. Did you ever hear of a piano-tuna?"

"Did you put fresh water into the fishbowl?"
"I didn't. The fish didn't finish the old water yet!"

"Did you wash the fish before cooking?"
"No. Why wash a fish that's lived in water all his life?"

"Waiter, I don't like the look of that codfish."
"Well, if you want looks, why don't you order a goldfish?"

Fishing

Last week I went fishing and all I got was a sunburn, poison ivy and mosquito bites.

There are two kinds of fishermen: those who fish for sport and those who catch something.

I used to fish through ice but all I ever got was cherries.

Then I caught a 220 pound tuna, but I had to throw it back. It was a piano tuner.

"Gee, dad, that's a swell fish you caught. Can I use it as bait?"

A thoughtful wife is one who has the pork chops ready when her husband comes home from a fishing trip.

I just met a fisherman who hadn't had a bite all day — so I bit him.

I'm always in luck when I go fishing. When the fish don't bite the mosquitoes do.

The only time a fisherman tells the truth is when he calls another fisherman a liar.

He spends his weekend fishing through ice — at the corner bar, looking for olives.

I like to go fishing because it gives me something to do while I'm not doing anything.

"Are you fishing?"
"No, just drowning worms."

"How did you come to fall into the water?"
"I didn't come to fall into the water. I came to fish."

"I'll tell you, it was that long. I never saw a fish like that!"
"I believe you."

"While fishing I spotted a whale."
"Nonsense. Who ever heard of a spotted whale?"

"Do fish grow fast?"
"Sure. Every time my Dad mentions the one that got away it grows another foot."

"Shame on you! A big man like you catching poor little helpless fish."
"Well, if the fish would keep their mouths shut, I wouldn't catch them."

"You have been watching me for three hours. Why don't you try fishing yourself?"
"I haven't got the patience."

Flies

I said, "Fly, fly," and the fly flew.

Why did the fly fly? A spider spied her.

There was a fly that was so upset it walked the ceiling all night.

"My, the flies are sure thick around here."
"Ah, I see you like them thin."

"I don't like the flies in here."
"Well, come around tomorrow, we'll have some new ones."

"I certainly don't like all these flies."
"Well, just pick out the one you like and I'll kill the rest."

"The offspring of a single fly may be in the millions."
"What, then, is the offspring of a married fly?"

"You want to work here? Can you shoe horses?"
"No, but I can shoo flies."

"If there are two flies in the kitchen, which one is the cowboy?"
"The one on the range."

Florida

I have to go to Florida for the winter. I can't afford an overcoat.

The temperature in Florida is in the 80's. 40 in the daytime and 40 at night.

He went to Florida and got a wonderful tan. Then he got the bill and turned white again.

There's so much money in Florida, people are coming back with green sunburns.

A friend of mine just came back from Florida with a wonderful tan. It cost him $16.75 a square inch.

"Is Florida really a good place for rheumatism?"
"Sure it is. That's where I got mine."

"You look so happy. What happened?"
"Wonderful news. My husband's had a breakdown and we have to go to Florida."

"I have come here for the winter."
"Well, you've come to the wrong place. There's no winter here."

Flowers

What does one send to a sick florist?

Some girls are like flowers. They grow wild in the woods.

If daughter is treated like a hothouse flower, she'll come home potted.

When a man brings his wife flowers for no reason — there's a reason!

A wallflower is a girl who wears a sweater to keep herself warm.

I'd like to buy some flowers for the woman I love, but my wife won't let me.

I used to wear a flower in my lapel but I had to give it up. The pot kept bumping against my stomach.

I like all kinds of flowers; wild, tame, and cauli.

A gift brought by men to wives to accompany a weak alibi.

"Why are flowers lazy?"
"They are always found in beds."

"What is the use of reindeer?"
"To make the flowers grow."

"What did the big rose say to the little rose?"
"Hiya, bud!"

"I don't give my girl cigarettes. She doesn't smoke."
"Give her flowers. She smells!"

"If April showers bring May flowers, what do Mayflowers bring?"
"Pilgrims."

"What flowers make you think of a kiss?"
"Tulips."

"What happened to that handsome man who sent you flowers every week?"
"He married the girl who sold him the flowers."

Food

To make pickles look like bananas, buy a can of yellow paint.

It's called a two-handed cheese. You eat it with one hand and hold your nose with the other.

She had a nervous breakdown trying to fit round tomatoes into square sandwiches.

The quickest way to make a tossed salad is to feed vegetables to a 18-month old child.

Appetizers are those little things you keep eating until you lose your appetite.

I never eat breakfast, I don't like to eat on an empty stomach.

Everything comes to him who orders hash.

I heard prices are going up. Pumpernickel is now Pumperdime.

There's one thing I can't eat for breakfast: supper.

"Shall we go the the Automat and liberate a few sandwiches?"

Nowadays, when you order a $5 steak you really get a mouthful.

When he eats, he eats! He always needs two credit cards to pay for his meal.

Every time I eat sugar I get a lump in my throat.

If a man eats dates, is he consuming time?

Mustard is no good without roast beef.

My friend is always swallowing razor blades. Perhaps he wants to sharpen his appetite.

I've been checking food prices for years. As soon as they get low enough, I'm going to buy some.

My wife is tired of planning meals. She just kicks the shelf at the foodmarket and takes whatever falls off.

The best thing to put in a homemade pie is your teeth.

If you wonder what your wife does with all the grocery money, stand sideways and look in the mirror.

When you have eaten onions, don't wear a rose in your button hole.

The best way to . . .

. . . cut your food bill in half is to use a scissor.

. . . eat cream cheese and lox is with a bagel.

. . . improve a vegetable dinner is with a big, juicy steak.

. . . keep rice from sticking together is to boil each grain separately.

. . . keep thin is not to exceed the feed limit.

. . . keep your foodbills down is to use a heavier paperweight.

. . . serve leftovers is to someone else.

. . . settle my wife's hash is with two spoonfuls of bicarbonate.

"What's the best thing to put in an ice cream soda?"
"A straw!"

"So you don't like corn on the cob?"
"No. That's why I bite it off."

"Why do you like gravy so much?"
"Because it has no bones."

"I heard you eat little food."
"That's right, because big food gets stuck in my throat."

"Do you like duck?"
"Duck is my favorite chicken, except turkey!"

"What did you have for breakfast this morning?"
"Oh, the usual argument."

"Why did he get angry when you ate a businessman's lunch?"
"I guess, he wanted to eat it himself."

"In this place you can eat dirt cheap."
"But who wants to eat dirt?"

"What's your favorite seafood?"
"Salt-water taffy."

"How do you like your steak, sir?"
"Big."

"I hate to say it, but this toast is quite tough."
"You're eating the paper plate, dear!"

"Doctor, do you approve of eating everything raw?"
"No, always wear clothes."

"You don't seem to realize which side your bread is buttered on."
"What does it matter? I eat both sides."

"How did you find the steak?"
"With a magnifying glass."

"What is your husband's favorite dish?"
"The blonde next door."

Fortune

Every time I open a fortune cookie I find a note inside from my wife telling me to come home at once.

Now I don't know what will happen to me. My fortune cookie contradicted my horoscope.

I lost my entire fortune when I misplaced my wallet.

He took his misfortune like a man. He blamed it on his wife.

My fortune teller informed me that I will go on a trip and meet good fortune. That can only mean that I'll find a parking place when I go downtown tomorrow.

To make a fortune today you have to come up with something that is low-priced, habit-forming, and tax deductible.

France

I'm glad I wasn't born in France because I can't speak a word of French.

Taking your wife to Paris is like taking a sandwich to a banquet

I don't speak much French. Just enough to have my face slapped.

In France the cops are so polite, I put my hand out for a left turn and a cop kissed it.

They laughed when I spoke to the waiter in French, but they didn't know I'd told him to give my friends the check.

"What part of London is in France?"
"The letter N."

"He speaks French like a native."
"Yes, like a native American."

"Were you in Paris on your vacation?"
"I don't know. My husband bought the tickets."

"How would you ask for water in Paris?"
"Who would drink water in Paris?"

"Did you have any difficulty with your French in Paris?"
"No, but the French people did."

"When I go to Paris should I bring you back a Matisse or a Picasso?"
"Well, I think all those French cars are almost alike."

Friendship

A friend in need is a drain on the pocketbook.

A friend in need is a friend to avoid.

A friend in need is a pest indeed.

A friend is a friend until he borrows money.

A friend not in need is a friend indeed.

Be kind to your friends. If it weren't for them you'd be a total stranger.

I misplaced our Christmas list. Now I haven't the slightest idea who our friends are.

If you have friends like him, you don't need enemies!

If you lend a friend five dollars and never see him again it was worth it.

It's easy to tell who your real friends are. They're the ones who stab you in the front.

My best friend married my sister. Now he hates me like a brother.

My best friend ran away with my wife and let me tell you, I'll miss him.

A real friend is the one who will visit you on a hot day even if you don't have air-conditioning.

Real friends are those who, when you've made a fool of yourself, don't feel that you have done a permanent job.

The best way to keep a friend is not to introduce him to anybody.

The best way to lose a friend is to tell him something for his own good.

The more arguments you win, the fewer friends you'll have.

The poor fellow has lost all his friends. All he has left are his relatives.

When a fellow needs a friend he often makes a mistake and gets a wife.

Never forget a friend, especially if he owes you money.

I had terrible luck. My best friend ran away without my wife.

There are two kinds of friends: those who are around when you need them, and those who are around when they need you.

She is one of my best friends. Why, I've known her ever since we were the same age.

"Lend me a dime. I want to call a friend."
"Here are two. Call both of them."

"Do you love your enemies?"
"Yes, all three of them – tobacco, women and liquor."

"You heard the saying: A friend in need is a friend indeed?"
"Yes, stranger."

"Don't you have any friends to play with?"
"Oh, I have friends, but I hate them!"

"Believe me, I pick my friends."
"Yes, to pieces!"

Fruit

The first pair ate the first apple.

It wasn't the apple on the tree that ruined Adam, it was the tomato on the ground.

She bought an apple and a lemon. The apple was a peach but the lemon was a lemon.

A little tomato who knows her onions can go out with an old potato and come home with a lot of lettuce and a couple of carats.

It was an apple that made Adam tell, and the same apple made Wilhelm Tell.

"But, doc, I eat lots of fruit. I have three cherries in every martini!"

"Why are you eating the banana with the skin on?"
"It's all right. I know what's inside."

"What have you in the shape of bananas today?"
"Cucumbers, lady."

"What kind of fruit is red when it is green?"
"Blackberry."

"What are you doing in my tree, young man?"
"One of your apples fell down and I'm putting it back."

"There's a lot of juice in this grapefruit."
"Yes, more than meets the eye."

"What did one banana say to the other?
"Let's peel!"

Furniture

I have antique furniture and a wife to match.

Everything in our kitchen is electrified — even the chairs.

Our furniture goes back to Louis XIV unless we pay Louis before the 14th.

We now have period furniture. We keep it for a period and then send it back.

Our house is furnished with period furniture. My wife sees something and says, "I want that – period!"

If my wife keeps buying Colonial furniture there's gonna be an American Revolution in my house.

My neighbor's furniture goes back to Louis XIV, while mine goes back to Sears Roebuck on the 15th.

Every time I see a four-poster bed I figure it's a lot of bunk.

The electric chair is period furniture because it ends a sentence.

Furniture is the other thing my wife likes to push around.

The furniture is so modern that the only time you're comfortable is when you sit on the floor.

By the time we have all the furniture paid for we'll have genuine antiques.

The most expensive piece of furniture in the world is a ringside table at a night club.

"What happened to your Morris chair?"
"Morris took it back."

"I saw you sitting in an outdoor cafe last night."
"What outdoor cafe? That was my furniture."

"I heard you bought some period furniture?"
"Yes, it went to pieces in a short period."

"I heard you are now selling furniture for a living. Any success?"
"So far I've sold only my own."

"We stand behind every bed we sell."
"Could you show me something else?"

Furs

When the wife wears the pants, some other woman wears the fur coat.

A new fur will do a lot for a girl and some girls will do a lot for a new fur.

I bought my wife a complete mink outfit. That's right – two steel traps and a rifle.

My wife's back gives me trouble. She wants it covered with a new fur coat.

We know a girl who said she'd do anything for a mink coat and now she can't button it.

I sure surprised my wife with a fur coat. She has never seen me in one.

There's nothing like a mink coat that gives a girl that warm feeling.

"Now I hope this mink will keep you warm — and quiet!"

She's so rich, she has a mink lining in her sable coat.

"That's a lovely fur coat. Did you kill it yourself?"

Now they have a wash-and-wear mink!

Behind every successful man is a woman who wants a mink coat.

My wife and I exchanged gifts. I gave her a beaver coat and she exchanged it for a mink coat.

G

Gambling

The last time I was in Las Vegas it was so crowded I had to go to a psychiatrist to find a place to lie down.

Gambling away the rent money is a moving experience.

After a gambler loses his shirt he can't expect to eat on the cuff.

This gambling place is so fancy, you have to wear a tie to lose your shirt.

But I did well in Las Vegas. Drove there in a $4,000 car and came back in a $20,000 bus.

The best way to beat the slot machine is with a sledge hammer.

No wonder Las Vegas is getting so crowded. Nobody has the plane fare to leave.

It is possible to come back from Las Vegas with a small fortune if you went there with a large one.

I go to Las Vegas every year to visit my money and leave a little interest there.

Money isn't everything, but if you stay in Las Vegas for a long time it's nothing.

I just hope they have more luck with my money than I did.

I lost my shirt in Las Vegas. I misplaced my laundry ticket.

I sure was lucky in Las Vegas. I forgot my wallet.

Las Vegas is a place where people stand around a big table waiting for their chips to come in.

Games

Playing cards can be expensive—so can any game where you are holding hands.

"Let's play house. You be the door and I'll slam you."

Tennis and golf are the only games you play without cards, except dominos!

Chess is a game that is played on squares by squares.

"What do you find the hardest thing to deal with?
"An old pack of cards."

"Why do you call your girl 'Checkers'?"
"Because she jumps whenever I make a wrong move."

"I see you have taken up chess and checkers."
"Yes, I found out these are the only games played on the square."

"So you have become an avid checker player."
"Yes, my doctor told me I needed some exercise."

Garbage

His idea of a big evening is to take out the garbage.

I was a garbage collector, and happy at my work. Then one day my cold cleared up.

Only in New York will a garbage collector wake you up at five in the morning and then forget to take away your garbage.

I don't need a garbage disposal. I throw my garbage out the window.

"John, the garbage man is here!"
"Tell him we don't need any today!"

"My husband is now a garbage collector."
"I see. Collecting garbage is now his bread and butter."

Gardens

Don't make the garden too big if your wife tires easily.

You can't do a good job in the garden of love with an old rake.

I had phenomenal luck with my garden this year — nothing came up.

The best time to spade the garden is right after your wife tells you to.

I always thought a yard was three feet until I started cutting the grass.

The grass may be greener on the other side of the fence but so is the water bill.

When buying a lawnmower you should select one that will last your wife several years.

"What is the first thing a gardener sets in his garden?"
"His foot."

"What do you grow in your garden?"
"Tired."

"What did the rake say to the hoe?"
"Hi, hoe!"

"Can I borrow your lawnmower?"
"He's not home yet!"

"Do you always water your garden with real Scotch?"
"Sure, I want stewed tomatoes."

"What runs around a garden but never moves?"
"A fence."

"What did your husband raise in his garden this summer?"
"Only his temper."

"Why are you jumping around in your garden?"
"I'm trying to raise mashed potatoes."

"Why should you never tell secrets in a vegetable garden?"
"Because the corns have ears."

"Is your mother home?"
"Do you suppose I'm mowing the lawn because the grass is too long?"

Gifts

Nothing lasts as long as a necktie you don't like.

She got a going-away present but she never did.

A gift shop is a place where they sell things you wouldn't have as a gift.

They divide gifts into two groups: those for wives and the more expensive items.

I bought her an Indian washing machine: a rock.

She got a 250-piece dinner-set for their wedding. A box of matches.

He's a man of rare gifts. Hasn't given one in years.

My boy wanted to go places so I bought him a chemistry set.

I gave her a 12-piece silver-set. Eleven dimes and a quarter.

I gave my wife a gift certificate and she exchanged it.

She wanted something for her neck, so I bought her a cake of soap.

Every time I buy a present she gets so excited! She can hardly wait to exchange it.

Then I gave her a pearl necklace. Of course, there was a string attached.

My wife has wedding presents she hasn't used yet. Like a broom, iron, vacuum cleaner . . ..

The best way to approach a woman with a past is with a present.

For her last birthday I bought her a plot in the cemetery – but she never used it.

I bought my wife a vacuum cleaner for her birthday, and now every year she gets another attachment.

I'm giving my wife a divorce – a gift that will last forever.

What to give to a man who has everything? A burglar alarm.

I once got a barometer made in Japan. Now I know when it's raining in Yokohama.

The perfect gift for a woman who returns everything is a boomerang.

I don't know what's wrong with me, but I still like getting gifts better than giving them.

"Oh, honey, you gave me just what I needed to exchange for what I wanted."

When in doubt about a gift, make it money; it's the easiest gift to exchange.

"I heard you bought a diamond ring for $1.50."
"Yes, without a stone."

"But why did you buy me such a small diamond?"
"I didn't want the glare to hurt your eyes."

"That's a nice wallet your wife gave you. Was there a bill in it?"
"Yes, the bill for the wallet."

"You never wear that lovely lingerie I gave you."
"Oh, I'm saving that for a windy day."

"What did you get your wife for her birthday?"
"A black robe. She reverses more decisions than the Supreme Court and she should dress accordingly."

"And what are you going to give your little brother for his birthday?"
"I don't know yet. Last year I gave him the measles."

"Why did you send me an empty box for my birthday?"
"At least when I send you nothing I wrap it up nicely."

Girls

A smart girl is one who knows how to play tennis, piano, and dumb.

A man can never tell about a girl until he is alone with her, and after that he shouldn't.

A green girl in pink condition can give a man the blues.

Anatomy is something everybody has but it looks better on a girl.

A tactful girl is one who makes a slow man think he is a wolf.

A good girl is good but a bad girl is better.

A good round sum will square things with most girls.

Any girl who knows how to cook can find a man who knows how to eat.

Beautiful girls don't bother me. I wish they would!

Every girl should know how to cook and clean the house. It will come in handy just in case she can't find a husband.

Every girl thinks she is different. That's why they're all alike.

Even if you can't read a girl like a book, it's nice to thumb the pages.

Funny, when a girl is old enough to go out alone, she doesn't.

Few things are more expensive than a girl who is free for the evening.

He didn't find any of her faults until he told her girl friend how lovely she was.

He met her in a revolving door and has been going around with her ever since.

"Is that your new girl or just the old one painted over?"

It is said when a girl with curves goes straight she is square.

It is true that opposites attract. A poor girl is always looking for a rich husband.

It isn't what a girl knows that bothers you. It's how well and where she learned it.

Just because a fellow prefers blondes, that doesn't make him a gentleman.

Just because a girl is well-oiled is no guarantee that she won't squeal.

"Your sister is spoiled, isn't she?"
"No, that's just the perfume she's wearing."

"Do you expect to find the perfect girl?"
"No, but it's lots of fun hunting."

"That blonde over there is a perfect picture of health."
"Yes, and the frame isn't bad either."

"Was that a new girl friend I saw you with last night?"
"No, just the old one painted over."

"She seems like a sensible girl."
"That's right. She won't pay any attention to me either."

"Do you have a parking problem with your new car?"
"Not with every girl."

"Who was that blonde I saw you with on Thursday?"
"That was the brunette you saw me with on Tuesday."

"Parden me, but you look like Helen Green."
"So what? I look worse in pink."

Golf

My golf is improving. Yesterday I hit the ball in one!

I shoot golf in the low 70's – until I get to the fifth hole.

I once missed a hole-in-one – by only five strokes.

A handicapped golfer is a man who plays with his boss.

By the time a man can afford to lose a ball, he can't hit that far.

His friends call it madness, but he calls it golf.

It's no sin to play golf on Sunday, but the way some play it's a crime.

I sure love golf. It makes me forget whom I'm married to, and whom I'm working for.

The way some Sunday golfers play, they're better off in church.

This golf course is so small, you don't holler "Fore!," you only holler "Three and a half!"

It's not that I really cheat at golf. I play for my health and a low score makes me feel better.

An important business executive will always talk golf at the office and business on the golf course.

A golfer can walk ten miles carrying his heavy golf clubs, but at home junior has to bring him the ashtray.

"I see your golf is improving. You are missing the ball much closer than you used to."

My wife told me, either I sell my golf clubs or we get a divorce.

Golf is a lot like business. You drive hard to get in the green and then wind up in the hole.

He's so dumb, when his friends asked him to come to shoot a round of golf, he took along his shotgun.

"Hello, dear. Wait till you see the dress I got to go with your new golf clubs!"

Did you hear about the golfer who cheated so much that when he got a hole-in-one he put down a zero on his score card?

How is it that a man can push a lawnmower for an hour and call it work, and when he pushes a golf cart all day he calls it recreation?

"Why do you play golf?"
"To aggravate myself!"

"My doctor told me I can't play golf."
"So he's played with you too?"

"Why is it hard to drive a golf ball?"
"Because it doesn't have a steering wheel."

"Why do you play so much golf?"
"My doctor said I must take my iron every day."

"I think golf is a rich man's game."
"Nonsense. Look at all the poor players!"

"What is really the secret of good golf?"
"To hit the ball hard, straight, and not too often!"

"I hear you play golf. What do you go 'round in?"
"Well, usually I wear a sweater."

"I heard you play golf. What's your handicap?"
"A wife and three children."

"Why do you wear two pairs of pants when you play golf?"
"In case I get a hole in one!"

"Well, daddy, how do you like my game?"
"I suppose it's all right. But I still prefer golf."

"Golf, golf, golf. I believe that if you spent a Sunday home I would die."
"But, honey, there's no use talking like that. You can't bribe me!"

Gossip

A gossip is a person who . . .

. . . always gets caught in her own mouth-trap.

. . . always gives the benefit of the dirt.

. . . always talks about things that make her speechless.

. . . believes much more than she hears.

. . . can give you all the details without knowing any of the facts.

. . . can keep the secret going.

. . . can't leave well enough alone.

. . . gets her best news from somebody who promised to keep a secret.

. . . has a good sense of rumor.

. . . has a small vocabulary but a large turnover.

. . . is always the knife of the party.

. . . is a newscaster without the sponsor.

. . . listens in haste and repeats in leisure.

. . . puts two and two together and makes five.

. . . suffers from acute indiscretion.

. . . tells everything she can get her ears on.

. . . tells things before you have a chance to tell them.

. . . turns an earful into a mouthful.

. . . would rather listen to dirt than sweep it.

More people are run down by gossip than by automobiles.

She doesn't like to repeat gossip, but what else can you do with it?

I will never repeat gossip, so please listen carefully the first time.

Her gossip is so interesting you always wish you would know the person she is talking about.

You shouldn't believe everything you hear but you can repeat everything.

It's really disgusting the way people go around telling terrible things about each other that are absolutely and completely true.

The most useless thing in the world is gossip that isn't worth repeating.

Talk about others and you're a gossip; talk about yourself and you're a bore.

Children would get less dirt in their ears if their parents wouldn't gossip in front of them.

Everyone should have at least two friends: one to talk to and one to talk about.

The difference between gossip and news is whether you hear it or tell it.

Gossip is like a grapefruit. In order to be really good, it has to be juicy.

She will never repeat gossip, but she will start it!

Gossip comes in three types: the vest-button type — always popping off; the vacuum cleaner type — always picking up dirt; the liniment type — always being rubbed in.

Government

Social Security is a system that guarantees you steak after your teeth are gone.

It's getting harder and harder to support the government in the style to which it has become accustomed.

Talk is cheap? Do you know what one session of Congress costs?

They ran him for Congress. It was the best way to get him out of town.

The government regards a citizen as one who has what it takes.

You can lead a man to Congress but you can't make him think.

They now have a President Doll: you wind it and for four years it does nothing.

Washington is a city where half the people wait to be discovered and the other half are afraid they will be.

H

Hair

I got a pocket comb but who wants to comb pockets?

He took a hammer along to the barber because he wanted his hair cut in bangs.

I call her "Tonic" because she always gets into my hair.

They now have a new type of wig for wearing in supermarkets. It has curlers in it.

When he said his right ear was warmer than his left ear I knew that his toupee was on crooked.

"You say, this is a camel's hair brush? It must have taken him an awful long time to brush himself."

She's got long black hair running down her back. Too bad it isn't on her head.

"I'd like to run my fingers through your hair. Can you remember where you left it?"

When she found her first gray hair she thought she had nothing to live for, so she dyed.

Most men regard blondes as golden opportunities.

Ever since I put grease on my hair, everything slips my mind.

My hair is so wavy people get seasick looking at it.

She looked like a doll. Her hair was pasted on.

Many a dumb blonde is really a smart brunette.

Many a bonde dyes by her own hand.

She has such beautiful hair, every time we go out I insist that she wears it.

Tell some girls their hair looks like a mop and they don't mind it. They don't know what a mop is.

A big advantage of being bald is that you can style your hair with a damp cloth.

"How can I avoid falling hair?"
"Jump out of its way."

"Do you like my hair in an upsweep?"
"No, where did you sweep it up?"

"This tonic will grow hair on a billiard ball."
"Who wants hair on a billiard ball?"

"How come you have such a long beard?"
"My brother left town ten years ago with my razor."

"Do you like my hair? I spent a long time over it."
"Indeed. I spend all my time under it."

"How do you like my new toupee?"
"Great! You can hardly tell it from a wig."

"I have a date with a girl and she doesn't know I wear a wig."
"Just keep it under your hat."

"I can't keep my hair in place."
"Why don't you remember where you put it?"

"What happened to the dopey blonde your husband used to run around with?"
"I dyed my hair."

"How did you lose your hair? Worrying?"
"Yes, worrying about losing my hair."

"I've decided to let my hair grow."
"How can you stop it?"

"Your wife's a blonde, isn't she?"
"I'm not sure. She just went to the beauty parlor."

Halloween

Is that your real face or are you still celebrating Halloween?

I like your dress but aren't you a little bit early for Halloween?

I won't say the girls were ugly at the Halloween party, but I danced with a pumpkin three times and never knew the difference.

"Don't look out the window, people will think it's already Halloween!"

She's so ugly she rents herself out for Halloween parties.

She's so ugly she's only allowed to walk the streets on Halloween.

She's so ugly she can walk the streets on Halloween without a mask.

Hands

Every time I try to hit a nail I hit my thumb.

Here is a girl with plenty of polish — on her fingernails.

You can burn your fingers trying to grab the toast of the town.

I thought she wore black gloves until she washed her hands.

She got her hands in everything — especially my pockets.

My hand measures nine inches. Three more inches and it would have been a foot.

I finally found the perfect way to get rid of dishpan hands. I let my husband do the dishes.

Pardon me, but I don't think your hand and my leg have been introduced.

If the palm of your hand itches, you're going to get something. If your head itches, you've got it.

Some men have submarine hands. A girl never knows where they'll turn up next.

He has very expressive hands. They move over you like an express.

Some girls are like paint. Get them stirred up and you can't get them off your hands.

Five years ago I asked for her hand and it's been in my pocket ever since.

I call my girl "Venus de Milo" because she always says "Hands off!"

When I asked her father for her hand he said, "Take the whole girl or nothing!"

She makes a living holding hands — she's a manicurist.

First I couldn't get her off my mind, now I can't get her off my hands.

A glove is something you keep one hand warm with while looking for its mate.

Don't bite your nails, especially if you are a carpenter.

Shaking your hand is like footprints in the sand of time.

It's much better to have your hands on a gal than a gal on your hands.

The best way to . . .

. . . avoid washing dishes is to have your husband eat out of your hands.

. . . drive a nail without smashing your fingers is to hold the hammer.

. . . stop hitting your thumb is to have your wife hold the nail.

"Have you any thumb tacks?"
"No, but I have some fingernails."

"May I hold your hand?"
"No, thanks. It isn't heavy."

"Take your hands out of your pocket."
"I can't. My suspenders broke."

"What do you mean I have baby hands."
"They are just beginning to creep."

"What's the matter with your finger?"
"I hit the wrong nail."

"Why don't you wash your hands?"
"What's the use, they'll only get dirty again."

"I'm seeking your daughter's hand, sir."
"You can always find it in my pocket."

"How did you get rid of your dishpan hands?"
"I got married again."

"How did you get the splinter in your finger?"
"I scratched my head."

"How can I keep my boyfriend's hands from getting rough?"
"Slap him."

"While you were in Paris, did you see the Venus de Milo?"
"See her? I shook hands with her."

"Why are your hands shaking?"
"I don't know. Maybe they're glad to see each other."

"I heard your friend had a finger in a big transportation deal."
"Yes, he thumbed a ride across the country."

Happiness

When a married man looks happy, we wonder why.

They lived happily until the day they got married.

But we've had a very happy marriage — now and then.

For twenty years my wife and I were very happy — then we met.

She's so happy because her boyfriend likes her husband.

I never knew happiness until I got married — then it was too late.

There's only one thing that keeps me from being happily married — my wife.

My friend just found happiness in the dictionary. It's under booze.

My wife is so happy that I'm not perfect. She loves to nag.

Some people cause happiness wherever they go. Others whenever they go.

A woman is really unhappy when she has a secret nobody wants to know.

I know we're going to be happy. She adores me and so do I.

They have been happily married for ten years. But not to each other.

I'm happy to live in a free country where man can do as his wife pleases.

Yes, my wife and I were married happily for five years. Then she lost her job.

I asked her to marry me and she said no! And we lived happily ever after.

Even if happiness could be bought there would still be those who would try to chisel on the price.

A woman gets married to make two people happy: herself and her mother.

They are a happy couple. He snores and she is deaf.

"Are you happily married?"
"Yes, for the sixth time!"

"Are you and your wife happy?"
"Oh, very happy. But let's talk about something cheerful."

"I think the poorest people are the happiest."
"Then marry me and we will be the happiest couple!"

"Say the word that will make me happy the rest of my life."
"Get lost!"

"Sonny, did you do your good deed today?"
"Sure did. First I went to see my aunt and she was happy and when I left she was happy again."

"Do you remember when you proposed to me? I was so overwhelmed that I didn't talk for an hour."
"Yes, honey. That was the happiest hour of my life!"

Hats

My wife's hats will never go out of style. They will always look silly.

There's nothing that goes to a woman's head faster than a new hat.

She is wearing one of those hats that looks like there was no mirror in the hat shop.

"Of course you can buy this hat, dear. I like that middle-aged look it gives you!"

A woman takes an hour to buy a hat that took 15 minutes to make.

Women's hats are all different because no one likes to make the same mistake twice.

A mirror is a thing in a hat store that makes you look foolish.

A hat designer decorated his new hats with live birds. Now, if you don't pay for the hat, it flies back to the store.

Her Easter hat had so many flowers on it, it came with a KEEP OFF sign.

If two women wearing the same hat smile at each other, they're twins!

Women who wear ridiculous hats are just trying to avoid being conspicuous.

Some men think women's hats are funny. Others have to pay for them.

I finally figured out a way to stop my wife from buying a new hat. Every time she sees one she likes, I say: "Oh, that's nice. My secretary has one just like it."

My wife bought a very useful hat. When she's not wearing it I clean the car with it.

"That hat fits you nicely."
"Yes, but what will happen if my ears get tired?"

"Does your husband confide in you about his business troubles?"
"Oh, yes, every time I come home with a new hat."

"I'd like to see something cheap in a straw hat."
"Put one on and look in the mirror!"

"Have you any blue neckties to match my eyes?"
"No, but we have some soft hats to match your head."

"Why did you buy this flower pot?"
"That's my new hat!"

"Why did you buy that hat?"
"Because I couldn't get it for nothing."

"When I saw you driving down the road, I guessed 55 at least."
"You're wrong, officer, it's only my hat that makes me look that old!"

"My treatments do you very good. You look much better today."
"But doctor, I always look better in this hat."

"You call that a hat, dear? I'll never stop laughing."
"You will when the bill arrives."

"What do you think would go well with my new hat, dear?"
"A blackout!"

"Your hat is on the wrong way."
"How do you know which way I'm going?"

"Darling, the woman next door got the same hat as I just bought. I'll have to buy another one."
"Well, I think it would be cheaper than moving."

"Why do you have this plaster over your eye, honey?"
"Plaster? That's my new hat!"

"Madam, your husband is lying unconscious in the hallway with a piece of paper in his hand and a large box at his side."
"Oh! I'm so happy! My new hat must have come."

Heads

The best way to get ahead is to have one.

The best way to get a good headache is to have too many drinks the night before.

I was going around with a girl until the revolving door hit me on the head.

He has so many wrinkles on his forehead he has to screw on his hat.

He had his head examined, but they couldn't find anything.

The only thing that seems to be able to stay in some people's heads longer than 12 hours is a cold.

I wish you were a headache. Then I could take an aspirin and you'd go away.

No wonder he has a cold. He has a hole in his head.

I was studying to be a bone specialist. Everybody said I had the head for it.

If there's an idea in his head it's in solitary confinement.

A man's problem while his wife is making a splash is to keep his head above the water.

Every time I take my wife to a restaurant she eats her head off. And she looks better that way.

A head is the only thing that a woman can keep under her hat.

Before TV nobody knew what a headache looked like.

If you want to see something swell, just hit your head with a baseball bat.

He's now a head adjuster. Drop in any time and have your head adjusted.

He is so bald his head keeps slipping off the pillow at night.

She can turn your head with flattery and your stomach with her cooking.

She went shopping all day but the only thing she got was a headache.

She has a vacant head, like the breakfast room at Niagara Falls.

I've got a lump on my head, but don't tell anybody. I want to keep it under my hat.

She has a good head on her shoulders, though it would look better on her neck.

"Do you have a headache or are you single?"

"Work hard and you'll get ahead."
"I've got a head."

"What do you take for a headache?"
"Liquor the night before."

"Can you stand on your head?"
"No, it's too high."

"I have a nagging headache."
"I didn't know you were married."

"I say, your son has a fine head."
"As good as new. Never been used."

"Why are you standing on your head?"
"I'm turning things over in my mind."

"Doc, will you give me something for my head?"
"Thanks, but I already have one."

Health

My wife's health has me worried. It's always good.

I'm in perfect health. In fact there's only one thing harder than my muscles: my arteries.

I drank to her health so often I ruined my own.

A girl who is the picture of health usually has a nice frame.

Every morning I get up at six and take a brisk walk to my vitamin bottle.

Some girls who are the picture of health are just painted that way.

I'm getting so accustomed to being tense that when I'm calm I get nervous.

People would be in better health if they didn't get sick so much.

He is so anemic, when a mosquito lands on him, all it gets is practice.

Some fellows can tear a telephone book in half. I've got trouble with a wet Kleenex.

This place is so healthy, they had to kill a guy to start a cemetery.

He was so strong he bent a spoon stirring the coffee.

He is so strong, he can tear a phone book in half the hard way — one page at a time.

The best way to stay in good health is not to get sick.

A little honey is good for your health — unless your wife finds out.

He has muscles in his arms like potatoes — mashed potatoes!

He is so tough, he eats sardines without removing the cans.

He is so tough, he uses a barbed wire for a hairnet.

He is so tough, he keeps his collar on with a nail in his back.

He is so tall, he has to stand on a chair to brush his teeth.

I get plenty of exercise. Every morning I pull the ice trays from the refrigerator.

"The man we just passed had a healthy look."
"Yes, and he's still looking."

"Has the doctor you're engaged to got any money?"
"He sure has. Did you think I was getting married for my health?"

"And how is your poor husband?"
"Yesterday he was enjoying poor health, but today he's complaining of feeling better."

Heart

She has a heart of gold: yellow and hard.

She has a big heart and a stomach to match.

She has a soft heart and a head to match.

She has a heart as big as a hippopotamus and a mouth to match.

Her heart belongs to me, but the rest of her goes out with other guys.

My heart belongs to daddy but my liver is my own.

She will serve a meal that will warm your heart. It will give you heartburn.

"You not only broke my heart by breaking up our engagement, you have also messed up my whole evening!"

Heat

IT WAS SO HOT, the cows were giving evaporated milk.

IT WAS SO HOT, I had to sleep with the air-conditioner under my pillow.

IT WAS SO HOT, we had to open the window to see the fire escape.

IT WAS SO HOT, we had to feed the chickens cracked ice to keep them from laying hard-boiled eggs.

IT WAS SO HOT, we couldn't stand it in the shade, so we walked out into the sun.

Hobbies

He has the craziest hobby. All day long he sits in the corner and collects dust.

Every husband should have a hobby, but don't let your wife find out about her.

A hobby is something you go goofy over to keep from going nuts over things in general.

A hobby is a type of hard work that you would be ashamed to do for a living.

Attending to your hobby is the little rest you get while your wife thinks up something for you to do.

A hobby is any work we don't have to do for a living.

He spends his spare time doing useful things, like walking down on UP escalators.

He likes to tinker around the house. In fact, his wife calls him the biggest tinker in town.

The first thing a man makes in his workshop is a mess.

My wife's hobby is making things — like mountains out of molehills.

A hobby is getting exhausted on your own time.

His hobby is collecting old echoes.

The best thing about a hobby is that it gives you something to do while your worrying.

Holidays

I sent my wife to the seashore for a holiday and what a holiday I had!

A holiday is a day a man stops doing what his boss wants and starts doing what his wife wants.

Besides Washington and Lincoln what other presidents happened to have been born on holidays?

He always starts on the 3rd to celebrate July 4th by buying a fifth.

If you want to have fireworks on the Fourth, try taking the day off to play golf!

Labor Day is a day when no one does any.

For Valentine's Day my wife baked me a pizza in a heart shape.

Hollywood

A Hollywood marriage is a good way to spend a weekend.

He just got in from Hollywood. Boy, what a walk!

I made a couple of pictures in Hollywood. But I had to stop – my Brownie broke.

A Hollywood couple has finally ironed out the divorce settlement. Now they can go ahead with the wedding.

There are beautiful girls in Hollywood. But I never see them. I work in a beauty parlor.

Here are two types of people: those who own swimming pools and those who can't keep their heads above water.

There is a Hollywood star who wanted to get a divorce in the same dress her mother got divorced in.

In Hollywood the last time some married couples see each other is at the wedding.

He went to Hollywood and made two pictures at the same time: his first and his last.

In Hollywood the girls are fit as a fiddle and ready to play.

The last picture I made in Hollywood, my producer told me, was the last picture I made in Hollywood.

A celebrity is one who works all his life in order to be well-known and then goes through back streets wearing dark glasses to avoid being recognized.

The man who invented slow motion movies got his idea while watching a Scotchman reach for a check in a restaurant.

I just returned from two weeks in Hollywood — looking for work.

Two movie studios are fighting for my services. The loser gets me.

They are a typical Hollywood couple. He is premature grey and she is temporarily blonde.

When a movie star is at liberty it means she's between marriages.

She wanted to marry a big movie star or nothing. She got her wish. Married a big nothing.

A Hollywood actress is always talking about her last picture or her next husband.

One Hollywood couple vowed to be true to each other — until after the honeymoon.

He just got a good offer from Hollywood. He's the only person who can play Frankenstein without make-up.

"I heard you made two movies in Hollywood."
"Yes, one from the front and one from the side."

"Have you ever been married before, madam? And if so, to whom?"
"What's this, a memory test?"

"I heard your friend is a big movie star. Is she married?"
"Occasionally."

"How long have you been married?"
"This time or all together?"

Honeymoons

After our honeymoon I felt like a new man. She said she did too.

I went alone on our honeymoon. My wife had already seen Niagara Falls.

The best way to save money on your honeymoon is to go alone.

He went alone on his honeymoon. He didn't believe in sleeping with a married woman.

They had to call off their honeymoon. Couldn't find a babysitter for two weeks.

I would have liked to take my wife along on our honeymoon, but she had to go to work the next day.

I took my wife to see a movie. It was the most time we'd spent together since our honeymoon.

She married so late in life that Medicare paid for the honeymoon.

He won't talk much about the honeymoon. All he said was, when they came down for breakfast the first morning, he asked for separate checks.

Our honeymoon was a long fight. My wife wanted to go to Bermuda and I wanted to go to Niagara Falls. We didn't speak to each other for two weeks. She was in Bermuda and I was in Niagara Falls.

Horses — Horseracing

I named my horse "Radish." Now I can say, "here's my horse Radish!"

There is nothing like horseback riding to make a person feel better off.

I think horsepower was much safer when only horses had it.

If you want your troubles off your mind, go horseback riding.

I told my wife, "Let me bet on one more horse and it'll be the last." It was.

The best way to stop a runaway horse is to bet on it.

I had a good day at the races. I didn't go.

This horse was so slow he was arrested for loitering.

I can shoe a horse. When I see a horse I go, "Shoo, shoo!"

I had a perfect system for winning at the races; then the track opened!

He promised me my horse would walk in; too bad the other horses were running.

I found a fine system to beat the first three races. Don't show up until the fourth.

I bet on a horse that went a mile and a quarter in two minutes. But when they took him out of his truck he didn't do so good.

Every time my horse runs they have to photograph the track to find him.

You can't make a fast buck on a slow horse.

The horse I bet on came in so late, he had to tiptoe into the barn not to wake the other horses.

"Why couldn't the pony talk?"
"He was a little horse."

"How do you make a slow racehorse fast?"
"Don't feed him!"

"What has four legs and flies?"
"A dead horse."

"Why are clouds like people riding horses?"
"Because they hold the rains."

"Why is a horse like a lollipop?"
"Because the more you lick it the faster it goes."

"Have you ever seen a horse that could count?"
"No, but I have seen a spelling bee."

"Would you shoot a horse with a wooden leg?"
"No, I'd shoot him with a gun."

Hospitals

A hospital is a place where people who are run down generally wind up.

What a swanky hospital that is. You have to be well before you can get in.

Although the patient had never been fatally ill before, he woke up dead.

What a hospital! Three o'clock in the morning they wake you up to give you a sleeping pill.

I was on pills and needles all week.

I got only one get-well card – from Blue Cross. It said: "Get Well Quick!"

It was so romantic. He proposed to her in the car and she accepted him in the hospital.

At my operation I laughed all the way through. My doctor had me in stitches.

Most hospitals have the recovery room in the wrong place. It should be near the cashier's office.

"Doctor, this is the third operating table you ruined this month. You must learn not to cut so deeply!"

"Nurse, I'm tired of nourishments. Bring me something to eat!"

Sure, hospital bills are high, but where else can you get breakfast in bed?

No patient should leave the hospital until he's strong enough to face the cashier.

"How can I get to the General Hospital fast?"
"Stand in the middle of this street for awhile."

"I heard they added a new wing to the hospital."
"They'll never get it off the ground."

"Would you like to see where I was operated on for appendicitis?"
"No, I hate to look at hospitals."

"I can't believe he's in a hospital. Why, only yesterday I saw him with a blonde."
"So did his wife."

"I heard your husband is in the hospital. What's the trouble?"
"It's his knee. I found a strange woman on it."

"How many beds should a hospital have?"
"At least one for each patient."

Hotels

Everything was cold in that hotel but the icewater.

Business is so bad, some hotels are stealing towels from the guests.

The lobby was so big they had *Burma Shave* signs on the way to the washrooms.

This hotel is so ritzy, when you request fresh milk they bring a cow into the dining room.

This hotel was so large by the time you walked from the reception desk to your room, you owed them for the first day.

When I asked for some hot towels, they advised me to put some cold ones on the radiator.

What a fancy hotel! I asked for something nice and restful for $30 and they gave me a sleeping tablet.

What a hotel! The elevator boys have two uniforms – one for going up and one for going down.

They advertised running water in every room, but I didn't expect it to come down from the ceiling.

The hotel was so dull, I sent down for another bible.

They wouldn't let you into the steamroom without tie and jacket.

This hotel was so swanky, even room service had an unlisted number

They changed the sheets twice a day — from one room to the other.

If you leave a call for six o'clock, they wake you at five just to tell you you have another hour to sleep.

This place is so fancy, you have to be shaved to enter the barbershop.

It's a very big hotel. To call the desk you dial long distance.

This hotel is only eight minutes from New York — by telephone.

I got a nice room with bath. Too bad they were in different buildings.

The clerk asked me if I had reservations. What do I look like, an Indian?

The bed was so hard, I had to get up twice during the night to get some rest.

This hotel was so swanky, you had to wash your clothes before you could bring them to the laundry.

They called it The Biltmore Hotel. It was built more like a stable.

This hotel has three lobbies. One for standing, one for sitting, and one for walking through.

I have never taken a hotel towel and I've got the silverware to prove it.

I had running water in my room. Too bad it never stopped running.

I couldn't complain about the elevator service. The elevator stopped right in the middle of my room.

I couldn't even complain about the room service. There wasn't any to complain about.

This hotel advertised "Bed and Board." I didn't know which was the bed and which was the board.

"Carry your bag, sir?"
"No, let her walk!"

"Room service? Can you send up a towel?"
"Please wait a minute, someone else is using it!"

"What are your weekly rates here?"
"I don't know. Nobody ever stayed that long."

"Does water always come through the roof in this place?"
"No, sir, only when it rains."

"But I would prefer a room with bath."
"This isn't your room, sir, this is the elevator!"

"Inside or outside room, sir?"
"Inside, it looks like rain."

"This is the house detective. You got a lady in there?"
"I don't know, I'll ask her."

"Did you stay at this hotel very long?"
"No, just long enough to hear their rates."

"Are the rooms here quiet?"
"Of course, sir. It's the people in them who are noisy.

"Do you have hot and cold water in this room?"
"Yes, sir, hot in summer and cold in winter."

"Do you want a room with shower?"
"I prefer a bed. I can't sleep in a shower."

"Is there any water in my room?"
"There was but we had the roof fixed."

"Why did you leave this hotel?"
"They only served three meals. Breakfast on Monday, lunch on Tuesday, and supper on Wednesday."

Houses

We live a quiet home life. I don't speak to her and she doesn't speak to me.

When the boarding house blew up, roomers were flying.

We have a real great toaster. Works on A.C. or D.C., but not on bread.

My cellar is so damp, when I laid a mousetrap I caught a herring.

We have one of those floor lamps with three degrees of brightness: dim, flicker and out.

We even have scream heat. If you want heat you have to scream for it.

It's really a waterproof house. After a rainfall not a drop leaks out of the cellar.

I'm a home-loving guy. And that's where I would like to be right now – home loving!

Our apartment is so small that the kitchen folds right into the wall when not in use.

After our wedding we looked like a new house. She was freshly painted and I was plastered.

Our new home is so far out in the country that our mailman sends our mail by mail.

Home is where you can say anything you like, because nobody pays any attention to you anyway.

I'm not saying our builder made a mistake, but who ever heard of going downstairs to the attic?

Our new house is so big, if you're in the living room and you gotta go, you can just about make it.

My husband is absolutely no good at fixing things, so everything in our house works.

"I passed your house yesterday."
"Thanks. I appreciate it."

"Does your wife like housework?"
"She likes to do nothing better."

"Do you run things in your house?"
"Sure, the vacuum cleaner and the washing machine."

"Do you have running water in your new house?"
"Only when it rains."

"Do you have hot and cold water in your place?"
"Sure, hot in summer and cold in winter."

"When will you straighten out the house, dear?"
"Why? Is it tilted?"

"How do you like my room as a whole?"
"As a hole it is all right. But as a room no good."

"Do these stairs take you to the second floor?"
"No, you'll have to walk."

"Weren't you ever homesick?"
"Not me. I never stay there that long."

"How far is your house from the station?"
"Only a ten minute walk if you run."

"Get out of here! This isn't your house."
"That's okay. I'm not myself tonight."

"This wall is so thin you can almost see through it."
"That's not a wall, that's the window!"

"I saw a big crowd in front of your house last night. What was up?"
"My window shade."

"You built that house wrong. You've got it upside down."
"No wonder I keep falling off the porch."

"Madam, this book will cut your housework in half."
"Good. I'll take two of them."

"I'm going to buy something nice in oil for the house."
"A landscape or a can of sardines?"

"May I take you home, honey?"
"Sure, where do you live?"

"What do you mean your house is damp?"
"There's too much due on it!"

"Are you a home-loving girl?"
"No, I can love anywhere."

"Can a man be in two places at the same time?"
"Certainly. I was staying in Ohio and was home-sick all the time."

"How much are they asking for your rent now?"
"About twice a week."

"I'll give you three days in which to pay your rent."
"All right. I'll pick Fourth of July, Christmas and Easter."

"When I left my last place the landlady cried."
"But I won't. You have to pay in advance."

"Do you have a basement in your house?"
"No, we only have a cellar."

Hunting

Then we went bear hunting and we were lucky. We didn't find any.

"How do you like my outfit? It's a hunting outfit. In fact, my brother is hunting for it."

This must be a good hunting spot. The sign says: FINE FOR HUNTING.

He likes to hunt mules. Gets a big kick out of it.

"Have you ever hunted bear?"
"No, but I've gone fishing in my shorts."

"I don't like the way you're holding your gun."
"Well, I don't aim to please."

"Well, I fired my gun and there was a dead lion at my feet."
"How long had he been dead?"

"Say, young man, what's the idea of hunting with last year's license?"
"Well, I'm only shooting at the birds I missed last year."

"Say, is there any good hunting in these parts?"
"There's plenty of hunting but very little finding."

"Sorry, sir, we have no ducks today. How about some chicken?"
"Don't be silly I can't tell my wife I shot a chicken, can I?"

Husbands

He looks like the first husband of a widow.

Many a poor husband was once a rich bachelor.

Her husband is an accountant but he can't figure her out.

A smart husband is one who thinks twice before saying nothing.

Whenever I meet a man who would make a good husband, he is.

A faithful husband is one whose alimony check is always on time.

More husbands would leave home if they knew how to pack their suitcases.

Often, a grouch a woman nurses is her husband.

Married men make the best husbands.

Why do husbands talk about their in-laws as if their wives didn't have any?

He is a model husband, but not a working model.

Her husband came in handy around the house until one day he came in unexpected.

They now have a gadget that does all the housework. It's called: Husband.

She trusts her husband everywhere because she goes everywhere with him.

I know a wife who tried so hard to please her butler, her husband quit.

This husband was so henpecked he had to wash and iron his own apron.

She used to work for her husband until she got him.

All husbands are alike, but they have different faces so you can tell them apart.

My husband has a split personality and I hate both of them.

A smart husband buys his wife very fine china so she won't trust him to wash it.

John is the sweetest, most wonderful husband in the world. Too bad I married Fred.

She is always after a husband and she doesn't care whose.

Husbands are like wood fires. When unattended, they go out.

The average husband knows where and when he got married. What escapes him is why.

The only time a husband is right is when he admits he's wrong.

"Is your husband hard to please?"
"I don't know. I never tried."

"Does your husband have a den?"
"No, he growls all over the house."

"Who's that lady with the little wart?"
"Keep quiet. That's her husband."

"What do you use for washing dishes?"
"Oh, I tried many things, but found my husband best."

"A husband like yours is hard to find."
"He still is."

"If you were my husband I'd give you poison."
"If I were your husband I'd take it."

"How long did you work for your husband?"
"Until I got him."

"I got a necktie for my husband."
"I wish I could make such a trade-in."

"Is your husband a weight watcher?"
"Yes, he watches every girl under 120 pounds."

"Does your husband go out much at night?"
"I don't know. I'll ask him the next time I see him."

"What makes you think your husband is getting tired of you?"
"He hasn't been home for seven years."

"I've got my husband to the point where he eats out of my hand."
"Saves a lot of dish washing, doesn't it?"

"How is it that you kept the same husband for five years?"
"His complexion matches my furniture."

"Here is a book: *How to Torture Your Husband.*"
"I don't need that. I have a system of my own."

"What kind of a husband do you think I should look for?"
"Better leave the husbands alone and look for a single man."

I

Insurance

My uncle took out $50,000 worth of life insurance, but it didn't do him any good. He died anyway.

I have a wonderful insurance policy. If I bump my head they pay me a lump sum.

Then there is the man who sells Imitation Fire Insurance to people who have imitation fireplaces.

Life insurance is something that keeps a poor man poor all his life so he can die rich.

Fun is like life insurance: the older you get the more it costs.

Last month I bought a retirement policy. All I've got to do is keep up the payments for 20 years and my salesman can retire.

Happy Heart Attack gives you double indemnity. If you die in an accident they bury you twice.

No one has insurance like the man who sells insurance.

"If you don't stop nagging me, I'll let my insurance lapse!"

They have a new Fire & Theft Insurance. But they only pay you if your house is robbed while it is burning.

I'm not saying I carry a lot of insurance, but when I go the company goes!

My house is thoroughly insured. For instance, if a burgler gets hurt while robbing my house, he can sue.

She was only an insurance man's daughter, but I liked her policy.

Blue Cross is a company that docks my pay to pay my doc.

In every insurance policy the big print giveth and the small print taketh away.

I thought my group insurance plan was fine until I found out I couldn't collect unless the whole group is sick.

I just bought a new life insurance policy but the small print is hard to understand. All I'm sure of is that after I die I can stop paying.

"Now that you're married, you should have some insurance."
"But why? My wife isn't dangerous."

"Was your late husband insured?"
"No, he was a total loss."

"Does your husband carry life insurance?"
"No, he carries fire insurance. He knows where he is going."

"While you were sick in bed, did your wife read to you?"
"Yes, my life insurance policy."

"Now dear, what will I get if I cook a dinner like that every day?"
"My life insurance."

"Didn't you know you can't sell insurance without a license?"
"I knew I wasn't selling any but I didn't know the reason."

"But lady, you can't collect life insurance on your husband. He isn't dead yet."
"I know that — but there's no life left in him!"

"In case I take out this life insurance on my husband and he dies tomorrow, what will I get?"
"Ten years."

"Honey, I just took out another $10,000 insurance policy."
"Oh, sweetheart, I could kill you!"

"Yes, this is the fire insurance office. May I help you?"
"Perhaps you can. My boss threatened to fire me and I want some insurance."

J

Jewelry

What a store! If you ask for a ring that costs less than $5000 — they look in the wastebasket.

My wife's diamonds once belonged to a millionaire: Mr. Woolworth.

The first thing to turn green in the spring is the Christmas jewelry.

The best way to stop your wife from spending too much money on gloves is to buy her a new diamond ring.

The most expensive jewelry is the wedding ring. It's already cost me $200 a month alimony.

Jokes

Old jokes never die, they just sound that way.

Many a joke sounds too good to be new.

He who laughs last doesn't get the joke.

If you can't laugh at the jokes of this age, laugh at the age of these jokes.

If your wife laughs at your jokes, it means that you either have a good joke or a good wife.

The oldest joke I know is, when Eve asked Adam: "Do you love me?" and he replied: "Who else?"

I hope you live to be as old as your jokes.

I know a joke about chocolate pie — it's rich!

I think we have company. I just heard mama laugh at one of daddy's jokes.

The pictures in the family album are fine, only they forgot to put some jokes under them.

Girls hate to hear jokes. I asked a girl to go for a walk with me in the woods and she said: "Don't make me laugh!"

Not all bum jokes are about hoboes.

Whenever I tell jokes, I get carried away!

A joke is a form of humor enjoyed by some and misunderstood by most.

Don't stop me if you have heard this joke. I want to hear it again.

The man who says his wife can't take a joke forgets himself.

I wonder if it hurts to crack a joke?

I could tell you some more jokes, but what's the use? You would only laugh at them.

My dentist got into trouble telling jokes. He pulled to many good ones.

I never heard a joke I didn't like.

He who laughs last usually has a tooth missing.

A wife laughs at her husband's jokes not because they are clever but because she is.

I'm not going to stand here and tell you a lot of old stale jokes, but I'll introduce the next speaker who will.

The man who doesn't laugh at a funny joke is probably not employed by the man who told it.

If you can't laugh at these jokes then put them in the stove and hear the fire roar.

Humor is a hole that lets the sawdust out of a stuffed shirt.

A joke is proof that the good don't die young.

Some women know their husband's jokes backwards — and tell them that way.

Always laugh heartily about your boss's jokes. He may be giving you a loyalty test.

A sense of humor is the ability to laugh at your own jokes when your wife tells them.

"Did you hear my last joke?"
"I sure hope so!"

"I will only marry a girl who can take a joke."
"What other kind could you get?"

"Did you hear the joke about the professor who showed his class two skulls of the same donor?"
"No, let's hear it!"

"I'll tell you a joke that will kill you."
"Please don't! I'm too young to die!"

K

Kissing

Wherever I go I take my wife along. I hate to kiss her good-bye.

Then she kissed me and I knew it was puppy love. Her nose was cold.

She is such a hot kisser she melts the gold in my teeth.

She gave me a kiss that would cost three dollars in a taxi.

Since my girl collects Green Stamps, all I get are sticky kisses.

She swears she's never been kissed. She can hardly be blamed for swearing.

He's kissed so many girls he could do it with his eyes closed.

When I get home my wife greets me with a dry martini and a wet kiss.

She looks at me as a brother. Every time I kiss her, she yells: "Oh, brother!"

A kiss over the phone is like a straw hat. It isn't felt.

I call my girl "Chesterfield" because her kisses satisfy.

A kiss that speaks volumes is seldom a first edition.

The best way to heat up a chicken is to kiss her.

Don't throw kisses unless the girl is a good catch.

Kissing is dangerous. I once kissed a married woman and got my nose flattened.

It is no fun kissing a girl over the phone unless you're right in the booth with her.

I'll always remember her kisses — every time I open the refrigerator.

"He hasn't actually kissed me yet, but he steamed my glasses a couple of times."

It is better to kiss a Miss than to miss a kiss.

Kissing a pretty girl is like opening a bottle of olives. After the first one the rest come easy.

A kiss is the shortest distance between two.

When they kiss and make up, she gets the kiss and he the make-up.

You can't kiss a girl unexpectedly — only sooner than she thought you would.

My girl uses paprika lipstick. Now her kisses burn like fire.

"Your kisses really burn."
"Maybe I oughta put out my cigarette?"

"I told you to stop kissing me."
"I did. Several times."

"What do you do when a girl faints?"
"I simply stop kissing her."

"Who told you that you could kiss me?"
"Everybody."

"Did he kiss you on the sly?"
"No, on the mouth."

"Am I the only girl you have ever kissed?"
"Yes, and by far the best looking."

"Who was that man I saw you kissing last night?"
"What time was it?"

"My wife kisses me only when she needs money?"
"Isn't it often enough?"

"I love your hair, your teeth, your lips . . ."
"Well then, kiss me and stop taking inventory."

"And will you always remember my kisses?"
"Yes, everytime I feel a chill."

"Girls run after my kisses."
"So what? After mine they are limp."

"Should a girl kiss with her eyes closed?"
"No, kiss him with your lips."

"She swears she's never been kissed."
"That's why she swears."

"I hear that kissing breeds disease."
"Let's start an epidemic."

"Am I the first girl you've ever kissed?"
"Might be — your face looks familiar."

"When I kiss a girl she knows she's been kissed."
"Who tells her?"

"Mother, is kissing dangerous?"
"Sure is. I got your father that way."

Knowledge

A wise man never blows his knows.

They say it pays to be ignorant. So how come I'm broke?

If ignorance is bliss, why aren't more people happy?

I would never buy an encyclopedia. My wife knows everything.

If my girl said what she thought she'd be speechless.

Everybody knows more than somebody, but nobody knows more than everybody.

"Remember, I may not be intelligent, but I'm far from smart!"

Any man who knows all the answers has most likely misunderstood the question.

I heard they shot the information clerk at the bus terminal. He knew too much.

All I know is what I read in the books I write.

Today's children know where babies come from. It's the birds and bees they don't know anything about.

"It's all right to be dumb, but you're making a career out of it."

"Say, how does Daylight Savings work? Do you move your clock up or down?"

Dumb? When I asked her to pass the plate, she said: "Upper or lower?"

Dumb? She would look for a wishbone in a soft-boiled egg.

Dumb? She couldn't tell which way an elevator was going if she had two guesses.

Dumb? The only thing she ever read was an eye-chart.

I finally had to move from Cincinnati. Couldn't spell it.

L

Language

I speak eight languages. Unfortunately I speak them all at the same time.

I speak three languages. Fair French, Good German and Great Britain.

I speak several languages but I can't master the tongue of my wife.

He's the only fellow who speaks Scotch with a soda accent.

They call our language the mother tongue because father seldom gets a chance to use it.

Kissing may be the language of love but money still does the talking.

The Chinese language only has about 15,000 words. But it's very difficult because none of them are English.

My girl is now showing an interest in foreign languages. She just asked for a French phone.

Girls shouldn't be allowed to study foreign languages. One tongue is enough for any woman.

The longest word in the English language is the one following the phrase: And now a word from our sponsor!

Sometimes studying languages gets ridiculous. I know a fellow who is beginning Finnish.

What's the use of speaking correct English? No one will understand you.

My wife always uses sign language. She signs for this and signs for that.

English is a funny language. A fat chance and a slim chance are the same thing.

"I'm now learning Spanish, but I'm having a little trouble with my vowels."
"Why don't you see a doctor?"

"I heard your daughter speaks Esperanto. Does she speak it fluently?"
"Just like a native!"

"You speak three languages?"
"Yes, Manhattan, Bronx and Brooklyn."

"Now say AH!"
"Ductor, noh speaka da English."

"He speaks Spanish like a native."
"Yes, like a native Hungarian."

"Can you read Chinese?"
"Only when it's printed in English."

"What speaks all the languages in the world?"
"An echo."

"They say that kisses are the language of love."
"Well, speak up!"

"Is there a word in the English language that contains all vowels?"
"Unquestionably."

Laughter

A wise man never laughs at his wife's old clothes.

He who laughs last is probably the one who intended to tell the story himself a little later.

"How can you look so clean and laugh so dirty?"

Keep smiling — it makes people wonder what you have been up to.

I like to see people smile and hear them laugh, but not when I'm changing a flat tire.

Laugh and the world laughs with you. Snore and you snore alone.

She laughed when I sat down to play. How was I to know that she was ticklish?

They laughed when I carried a bag of water to the dance floor. They didn't know I was going to swing it.

They laughed when I made a new kind of dynamite, but when I dropped it, they exploded.

They laughed when I put Iodine on my paycheck. They didn't know I got a cut.

They laughed when I sat down at the piano. I had forgotten to bring a stool.

They laughed when I walked over to the piano — but they were right. I couldn't lift it.

They laughed when I picked up the violin. They didn't know I was from the finance company.

"Have you ever had a great laugh?"
"Yes, the first time I saw you."

"Did anyone laugh when you fell on the ice?"
"No, but the ice made some bad cracks."

Laundry

A laundry is a place where your clothes are worn out.

I've got a shirt with a turned-down collar. It's been turned down by every laundry.

I keep getting my laundry back the same day. They keep refusing it.

Then I opened a hand laundry. But most people wanted to wash their own hands.

You ought to see how nice and white my shirts come back — even the green ones.

Now I have to change my laundry. Last week they lost the buttonholes from my shirts.

I promised my laundry I'd give them back all those pins if they'd give me back all my buttons.

I gave my wife a laundry dryer for her birthday — 50 feet of clothesline.

My new laundry never lost a single button. Sleeves, yes, but never a button.

I feel like a changed man. My laundry came back.

My wife thinks a wishy-washy is a Chinese laundryman.

A laundry is a place where clothes are mangled.

"You haven't changed much."
"No, my laundry is on strike."

"Who does your laundry?"
"Nobody, I tear the buttons off myself."

"Why does your laundry put so many pins in your shirts?"
"Well, something's got to hold them together."

"George hasn't changed in 20 years."
"He must have saved a lot on laundry bills."

Law — Lawyers

There is one law we don't have to enforce — the law of gravity.

If you can't get a lawyer who knows the law, get one who knows the judge.

The law gives me the right to open my wife's mail, but not the courage.

What a lawyer! He once got a jury so confused, they sent the judge to jail.

I think my father was a lawyer. When he saw me the first time he said: "I object!"

There was a lawyer who joined the nudist colony. He never had a suit again.

I heard we have 35 million laws to enforce the Ten Commandments.

I'm trying to be a good lawyer. I even built myself a bar to practice behind.

That persistant lawyer spent a whole evening trying to break a girl's will.

Sometimes the law of gravity doesn't work. It's easier to pick up a girl than to drop her.

Nowadays a thoughtful girl saves a piece of her wedding cake for her divorce lawyer.

He is a real lawyer. In fact, he even named his daughter Sue.

She is a female private eye — sort of a slick chick dick.

"Do you have a criminal lawyer in town?"
"Well we think so, but we can't prove it!"

"Why did the client bring clothes to the lawyer?"
"Because he lost his suit."

Client: "My husband has flat feet. Can I get a divorce on that charge?"
Lawyer: "Not unless his feet visit the wrong flat."

Lawyer, over the phone: "They can't put you in jail for that!"
Client: "Oh, yeah? Where do you think I'm calling you from? The Public library?"

"As your attorney, I couldn't do any more for you."
"Thanks. Ten years were plenty!"

Laziness

She only uses drip-dry dishes.

The only thing he can do fast is get tired.

His self-winding watch is three days slow.

It takes her five minutes to boil a three-minute egg.

Even when his ship would come in, he wouldn't bother to unload it.

Even his nose is lazy. It won't even run when he has a cold.

She is so lazy, she washes her dishes in bed.

The only thing she ever made was mistakes and cigarette ashes.

"Is your wife lazy?"
"Everything but her tongue!"

"Why are tall people always the laziest?"
"Because they are longer in bed than short people."

"You got to hand it to John when it comes to petting."
"Why? Is he that lazy?"

"There's nothing wrong with you. You're only lazy."
"Now, Doctor, give me the medical term so I can tell my wife."

Legs

Every time I put my foot down my wife steps on it.

I'm so busy, I bought two desks. One for each foot.

Footprints in the sand of time are not made sitting down.

"Why don't you sit down and take a mess off your feet?"

His feet have been known to fall asleep while he was running after a bus.

A girl who keeps on her toes keeps away from heels.

My wife bought me a garden spade. Now I have a place to put my foot down.

She's got a very unusual figure. Her seams are straight but her legs are crooked.

The best way to stamp out a hot foot is to step into a puddle.

Among the things that run in all families are stockings.

Stockings are things that run while a woman is walking.

A lot of husbands suffer from cold feet, but not always their own.

There are twice as many feet in the world as there are people.

Never let grass grow under your feet. It tickles!

Now they've got a chlorophyll foot powder. Makes your feet kissing sweet.

Some girls are not afraid of mice. Others have pretty legs.

He had such big feet, they used him to stamp out forest fires.

Here is a fellow with flat feet and a head to match.

I never could get shoes that match until I found out why. My feet don't match.

He is very polite. Always takes his shoes off before putting his feet on the table.

Mom broke a leg. Now dad can't work. She broke his leg.

She has musical feet — two flats.

Dad is always bothered by flat feet. They keep giving him speeding tickets.

Get a load of her legs! I've seen better-looking bones in soup.

If you haven't a leg to stand on it's smarter not to kick.

A girl with cold feet does a lot of walking.

She had such bony knees, every time she sat down her knees made a fist.

Just because you have legs like a canary doesn't mean you're a singer.

"How much are your four-dollar shoes?"
"Two dollars a foot."

"Keep your feet where they belong!"
"Don't tempt me!"

"My uncle has a cedar chest."
"My uncle has a wooden leg."

"Doc, I have a sharp pain in my left leg."
"Try walking on the other foot."

"My girl's legs are without equal."
"You mean they know no parallel."

"Doc, what can I do about my broken leg?"
"Limp."

"You have your shoes on the wrong feet."
"But these are the only feet I have."

"Darling, your stockings are wrinkled."
"I'm not wearing any."

"The pain in your leg is caused by old age."
"But Doctor, my other leg is the same age and it doesn't hurt!"

"There's a man outside with a wooden leg named Smith."
"What's the name of the other leg?"

Letters

Today I wrote three letters: A, B and C.

He is a man of letters. He works for the post office.

I don't mind my wife finding the letters I forgot to mail. I just don't want her to find the letters I forgot to burn.

The nicest thing about dictating a letter is that you can use words you don't know how to spell.

Libraries

How can you whistle while you work if you are a librarian?

What a library. I owed them two cents on a book so they attached my salary.

My library consists of books that I have that nobody wants to borrow.

I have a very colorful library. Five books are red, some are green and a few are brown.

"Who told you that you're a good bookkeeper?"
"The librarian."

"My little brother fell into a manhole. What shall I do?"
"Run to the library and get a book on how to raise a child."

"My father always gives me a book on my birthday."
"What a wonderful library you must have."

"I want some current literature."
"Here are some books on electric lightning."

My husband has so many books in the house, every time I enter I have to show a library card.

Licenses

A marriage license costs only three dollars down and your income for life.

A marriage license is really a hunting license for one dear only!

When you're run down, the best thing to take is the license number.

"Your driving license seems okay. Now, suppose you tell me how you got it?"

Every year he goes down to City Hall to see if his marriage license has expired.

She's been married so many times they don't give her a license anymore, they just punch the old one.

Nothing improves a man's driving like the sudden discovery that his license has expired.

My husband keeps reading the marriage license — searching for a loophole.

Life — Living

There's no use worrying about life because nobody gets out alive.

"What are you doing for a living? You *are* living, aren't you?"

Life is like a shower. One wrong turn and you're in hot water.

My life is so uneventful, I have to count sheep to keep awake.

These days a man can't afford to make a living.

Many a woman marries a man for life and then finds out he doesn't have any.

There's one good thing about life. It's only temporary.

You can't make a hit if you have no aim in life.

When life hands you a lemon, make lemonade!

Life is really wonderful, don't miss it if you can.

He's a real genius. Can do anything but make a living.

Cost of living: income plus ten percent.

Life begins at 40, but you will miss a lot of fun if you wait that long.

She gave me the best years of her life. Now come the worst years.

We have the highest standard of living in the world. Too bad we can't afford it.

He is so conceited, he always sings: "The best things in life are me!"

She was having the time of her life until her husband found out.

We ought to be thankful we have the means to live beyond.

It's easy to make money. It's just hard to make a living.

Living a double life will get you nowhere twice as fast.

It is almost foolish to pay what it costs to live nowadays.

She goes through life standing at the complaint counter.

The other night, while lying on the couch, I reviewed the high point of my life and fell asleep!

"It costs me $5000 to live."
"Don't pay it. It's not worth it."

"Did you live here all your life?"
"I don't know. I haven't died yet."

"I guess we all just live and learn."
"Yes, but you just live."

"You live in Fishhook? Where is that?"
"At the end of the line."

"What do you do for a living?"
"As little as possible."

"Is life really worth living?"
"What else can you do with it?"

"What is the reason women live longer than men?"
"They have no wives."

"I gave you the best years of my life!"
"Those were the best?"

"How can you live without a wife?"
"Much cheaper."

"I gave you the best years of my life!"
"So what do you want? A receipt?"

"I live by my wits."
"Now I know why you look so hungry."

"This is a dangerous world we live in."
"Yes, very few get out of it alive."

"Your money or your life!"
"Take my life. I'm saving my money for old age."

"How long can a man live without a brain?"
"I don't know. How old are you?"

"I wonder if I shall ever live to be 100."
"Not if you remain 25 much longer."

"Do you live within your income?"
"Oh, no. All I can do is live within my credit."

Abraham Lincoln

I always celebrate Lincoln's Birthday by going through his tunnel. It's not easy since I haven't got a car.

The stores were so crowded on Lincoln's Birthday that I bought my own tie three times.

They say Lincoln wrote his homework on a shovel. I wonder how he ever got it in the typewriter.

They say that Lincoln wrote the Gettysburg Address while riding from Washington to Gettysburg on an envelope.

"Say, do you know Lincoln's Gettysburg Address?"
"No, I didn't know he had moved."

"Have you ever read Lincoln's Gettysburg Address?"
"No, I'll wait till they make a movie out of it."

"Don't you want to grow up and be like Lincoln?"
"No, who wants to be a tunnel?"

"George, can you give me the Lincoln's Gettysburg Address?"
"No, but I think he used to live in the White House in Washington."

Lingerie

I gave her a sheer negligee and she let me put it on. But I don't look good in a sheer negligee.

A girdle is a device that holds a girl in when she's going out.

She ordered a bra by mail. Now she waits for her shape to come in.

She kept complaining that I never give her anything, so I bought her a girdle. That ought to hold her.

A girdle doesn't change a woman's weight. It only moves it to a more interesting location.

A girdle is a device to keep an unfortunate situation from spreading.

Now she's wearing a girdle with a window in it. Her doctor told her to watch her stomach.

Women wear girdles from instinct — a natural desire to be squeezed.

A girdle is the difference between facts and figures.

Women who cannot afford a new girdle make the old one stretch.

A woman has reached middle-age when her girdle pinches her and her husband doesn't.

She keeps her money in her girdle. It's the only way she can stretch it.

They have now a new girdle, called the "Irish Girdle." They are so tight, you'll turn green.

Lions

The lions were so fierce that when the tamer went into the cage with a chair he didn't get a chance to sit down.

If I ever come face to face with a lion, I know just what steps to take: long ones!

The best way to talk to a lion is by long distance.

"Have you ever seen a man-eating lion?"
"No, but I have seen a man eating herring."

"What do you do when you see a big lion?"
"Hope he doesn't see me."

"Are you the celebrated lion tamer?"
"No, I only comb the lion's hair and clean his teeth."

"Do you know how to stop a lion from charging?"
"Sure. Take away his credit card."

"Look, guide, here are some lion tracks."
"Fine. You see where they go and I'll find out where they came from."

Losers

You think you have troubles? My sun-dial is slow!

All he ever gets on a silver platter is tarnish.

The only break he ever got was a coffee-break.

When he carried his young bride over the threshold, he got a hernia.

His swimming pool burned down.

Every time . . .

. . . it rains I have no umbrella.

. . . it rains soup I have only a fork in my hand.

. . . my ship comes in there is a dock strike.

. . . my wife has an accident in the kitchen I get it for dinner.

. . . my wife buys some doughnuts she takes the dough and I get the nuts.

He is such a loser . . .

. . . his artificial flower died.

. . . his goldfish looks like him.

. . . he bought some stock at 12 and it went down 15 points.

. . . even if he played Bingo alone he wouldn't win.

. . . health food makes him sick.

. . . aspirin gives him a headache.

Love

I love her for what she is – rich.

"I love you. Next to me I love you best."

The stove was cold and so was his wife.

The best way to hold a man is in your arms.

"Let's fight, so we can kiss and make up!"

Love is an itch around the heart that you can't scratch.

It was love at first sight. Then I took a second look.

"If you really loved me, you would have married someone else!"

She always flirts with the butcher. Playing for bigger steaks.

Here's to the man who loves me terribly. May he soon improve.

Last night we had an argument. She doesn't like the way I feel about her.

What a wonderful night. The moon was out and so were his parents.

Romance goes out the window when she stops knitting and starts needling.

It's love when she sinks in his arms and ends up with her arms in her sink.

He loved her so much he worshipped the ground her father struck oil on.

Some people love to go to the movies. And some people go to the movies to love.

Love is like photographic film. It has to be developed in the dark.

"I love you terribly."
"You certainly do."

"How much do you love me?"
"How much do you need today?"

"Are you fond of nuts?"
"Is this a proposal?"

"Say you love me! Say you love me!"
"You love me!"

"I love you and I could die for you!"
"How soon?"

"What makes you think they are engaged?"
"She has a ring and he is broke."

"Why did you break your engagement."
"Because he wanted to get married."

"Darling, how can I ever leave you?"
"By bus, taxi, streetcar or subway."

"Did you miss me while I was gone?"
"Were you gone?"

"What do you know about love?"
"Plenty. I drove a taxi for five years."

"Men don't interest me. I said no to many of them."
"What were they selling?"

"Doris became engaged to an X-Ray technician."
"I wonder what he sees in her?"

"Frank's in love."
"That's nothing. Hoboken is in New Jersey."

"If we become engaged, will you give me a ring?"
"Sure, what's your phone number?"

"Will you love me when I'm old and gray?"
"Why must I wait that long?"

"Jack makes me tired."
"It's your own fault. Stop running after him."

Luck

Last week I had terrible luck. My chauffeur ran away with my wife.

I'm lucky. I have a wife and a cigarette lighter and both are working.

I have bad luck. Every time I meet a married woman she's got a husband.

I'm so unlucky. Bought a suit with two pairs of pants and burned a hole in my jacket.

I've had bad luck with both my wives. The first divorced me and the second won't.

It is sure hard luck being shipwrecked on a desert with your own wife.

Bad luck is bending over to pick up a four-leaf clover and being infected by poison ivy.

He had bad luck all his life, but when they dug his grave, they struck oil.

"Do you think I'll lose my looks as I get older?"
"If you're lucky."

"My wife took everything and left me."
"You're lucky. Mine didn't leave."

"My wife doesn't know what she wants."
"You're lucky. My wife does."

"I have no luck with women."
"Lucky fellow!"

M

Man

An unmarried man has no buttons on his shirt. A married man has no shirt.

The trouble with most men is they know all about women but nothing about wives.

Never hit a man when he is down. He might get up again.

Some men can't think straight. They always have curves on their mind.

A wise man is one who is smarter than he thinks he is.

Man's troubles are due to three things: women, money, and both.

Men are fools to marry women, but what else can they marry?

All men are not homeless, but some are home less than others.

Some men need two women in their life. A secretary to take things down, and a wife to pick things up.

When a man is always late for dinner, either his wife is a poor cook, or he has a pretty secretary.

Married men make the best salesmen because they are used to taking orders.

Even if a man could understand women, he still wouldn't believe it.

Every man should have a wife — preferably his own.

Modern man will stand for anything — except a woman on the bus.

Behind every famous man is a woman who says there is a woman behind every famous man.

By the time most men learn how to behave themselves, they are too old to do anything else.

"I'm a self-made man."
"We accept your apology."

"Men are all alike."
"Yes, men are all I like."

"Do smart men make good husbands?"
"Smart men don't get married."

"I heard your wife is a wonderful judge of men."
"Yes, she can tell a man from a woman every time!"

"I know a man who says he can't sit down and he can't stand up."
"Well, if he tells the truth, he lies."

"Men are all alike, aren't they?"
"Yes, every one you meet is different."

Marriage

Isn't marriage wonderful? To be able to sit in your own home, relax, drink beer and all night watch your wife's favorite programs.

My ambition is to marry a rich girl who is too proud to let her husband work.

Before we got married my wife promised to sew, clean and cook, and she did. She sowed her wild oats, cleaned me out, and cooked my goose.

I was married for five years and never told anybody. I like to keep my troubles to myself.

He acquired a large vocabulary — he got married.

I asked her to marry me so she put me on her wedding list.

And they said their marriage wouldn't last. They left the church together didn't they?

My marriage is a continuous process of getting used to things I hadn't expected.

It's a give-and-take marriage. He gives and she takes.

We're equal partners in our marriage. I'm the silent one.

In all the years I'm married I never stopped being romantic. If my wife ever finds out, I'm dead.

She's been married so many times the wedding dress is her native costume.

Aren't they a lovely couple? He's willing to die for her and she's willing to let him.

I was crazy to get married, but I didn't realize it at the time.

Before we got married I caught her in my arms. Now I catch her in my pockets.

She didn't want to marry him for his money but it was the only way she could get it.

All marriages are happy. It's the living together afterwards that causes all the trouble.

A man knows he is married when his wife puts a dent in his bank account and one in his car.

When they got married it wasn't by the Justice of Peace, it was by the Secretary of War.

Always get married early in the morning. That way if it doesn't work out, you haven't wasted the whole day.

Marrying a woman for her beauty is like buying a house for its paint.

When my old flame walked into my married life we had a big explosion.

"Are you married?"
"No, I was hit by a car."

"Would you buy a letter opener?"
"Buy one? I married one!"

"They say Smith is getting married."
"Serves him right. I never liked that fellow."

"How much does it cost to get married, Pop?"
"I don't know. I'm still paying for it."

"I heard you got a new dishwasher."
"Yes, I got married again."

"Would you marry the biggest fool on earth?"
"Oh, John, that comes so sudden."

"I can't go out tonight with you. I'm getting married."
"Well, how about tomorrow night?"

"Darling, today we are married 12 months."
"It seems more like a year to me."

"I don't intend to be married until I'm 30."
"I don't intend to be 30 until I'm married."

"You're the last man I ever expect to marry."
"How many are there ahead of me?"

"You're wearing your wedding ring on the wrong finger."
"I know. I married the wrong man."

"How can I get a wart off my hand?"
"Shoot him or marry him!"

"Marry my daughter? Why? She is only a girl!"
"I know. That's why I want to marry her."

"Is Bill's marriage a happy one?"
"I think so. He was still smiling when he left the church."

"I'm getting married next week."
"Against whom?"

"Are you married?"
"No, but I'm happily divorced."

Memory

Memory is the thing we forget with.

To improve your memory, lend people money.

He reminds me of a toothache I once had.

I'll never forget the day I first met my wife, although Heaven knows I've tried.

I always remember faces I never saw before.

"I'm sure we've met. I can't remember your name, but I never forget a dress."

She was one of the best girls I ever loved — but I can't remember which one.

My wife has a terrible memory. She doesn't forget anything.

The best way to remember something is to try and forget it.

Memory is what tells a man his wedding anniversary was yesterday.

He is so old, he still chases women but can't remember why.

Memory is what keeps telling you you know that fellow without giving you any idea who he is.

He remembers his social security number, his area code and his bank account number, but always forgets which is which.

Memory is that thing which reminds us we have forgotten something which we can't remember.

My memory is excellent. There are only three things I can't remember. I can't remember faces, and I can't remember names and, now I have forgotten the third thing.

It's better to have nothing to remember than nothing to forget.

Writing things down is the best secret of a good memory.

"Have you forgotten that you owe me five dollars?"
"No, not yet. Give me time and I will."

"Doctor, I'm losing my memory."
"Oh, forget it!"

"Have you forgotten?"
"No, I have three gotten!"

"You promised to forgive and forget."
"Yes, however, I didn't want you to forget that I have forgiven and forgotten!"

"I used to be young once."
"What memory — what memory!"

"I have forgotten more than you will ever know."
"I would rather know what you have forgotten than what you remember."

"You have got a good memory, but it's too short."

"We must separate. Just try to forget me."
"I can't. I'm a memory expert."

Miami Beach

It was so hot in Miami Beach the women didn't carry their minks, only the appraisals.

It was so hot in Miami Beach, one woman almost died. Luckily a life guard opened her mink coat just in time.

They say it's 80 in Miami Beach. Is that the temperature or the room rate?

Next week I'm going to Miami Beach for my health. That's where I left it last year.

The Mind

He is a mental tourist. His mind wanders.

A man who cannot make up his mind probably has no mind to make up.

People with open minds should wear warm hats.

Having a hole in the head doesn't always indicate an open mind.

Many people think they have an open mind when it is really their mouth.

He went to a mind reader the other day and was only charged half price.

He's got a photographic mind. Too bad it never developed.

He has a mechanical mind but he keeps forgetting to wind it up.

I had my mind made up to stay home with her, but she had her face made up to go out.

I don't know what to do. My heart says yes, my mind says no, and I haven't heard from my liver yet.

Her mind is a closed book, and what's worse, it comes in an awfully plain wrapper.

If you wish to broaden your mind, place a stick of dynamite in each ear and put your head in the barbecue.

He has such a low mind he wears his socks to bed to keep his neck warm.

If you have half a mind to get married, do it. That is all it takes.

A smart woman always asks her husband's opinion after she has made up her mind.

People who don't mind their own business either have no mind or no business.

"My mind is made up. Don't confuse me with the facts!"

She has a narrow waist and a broad mind.

The best way to change a woman's mind is to agree with her.

He wanted to be open minded so he blew his brains out.

His mind is so small it would ruin your eyes trying to read it.

"I have changed my mind."
"Thank heaven! Does it work better now?"

"Darling, my mind seems to wander."
"Don't worry. It's too weak to go very far."

"Darling, they say that too much kissing affects the mind."
"You're crazy!"

"I've got a mind of my own."
"Why don't you bring it around sometimes?"

"I'm going to give you a piece of my mind."
"Watch out now. You don't have much left."

"What is never seen but often changed?"
"Your mind."

Mini-Skirts

She is wearing a mini-skirt over her maxi shape.

The only thing a mini-skirt does for her is give her cold knees.

If her dress were any shorter it would be a collar.

She was so short, her mini-skirt dragged on the floor.

She doesn't have the legs for mini-skirts, only the nerve.

There are now three kinds of mini-skirts: mini, micro and don't bend over.

Those mini-skirts get higher and higher. I wonder where they will stop?

The skirts are getting shorter and the neckline lower. I'd like to be there when they meet.

If she wears her dress any lower she would be barefoot all over.

"Do you think mini-skirts will draw more interest than savings accounts this year?"

Mini-skirts always get maxi-attention.

When my wife wears one of her mini-skirts men turn to look the other way.

Mini-skirts are like the cost of living: neither can go much higher.

Money

She spends money like it is going out of style.

I earn roughly $200. When you smooth it out it is almost $25.50.

My wife's got everything and I only wish I could get some of it back.

Money doesn't talk these days. It goes without saying.

My wife throws away money like it was an anchor.

The other fellow's wallet always looks greener.

Every time I drop a dime it's my last one.

Whenever I need cash I visit my uncle. He's the kin I love to touch.

She has everything credit can buy.

They say you can't take it with you. I can't even afford to go.

When your outgo exceeds your income, then your upkeep is your downfall.

By the time a man is rich enough to sleep late, he's too old to enjoy it.

I wouldn't sell my place for all the tea in China — but for cash, any time!

Show me a man with a million dollars and I'll show you a man who's rich.

Money is called legal tender, but when you don't have it, it's tough.

I've got enough money to last me a lifetime, unless I buy something.

Behind every successful man stands a woman with a handful of bills.

It is easy to meet expenses. Just turn around and there they are.

I'm saving my money. Some day it may be worth something.

Money talks, but it doesn't say when it's coming back.

There is still one thing that you can get for a penny: your weight.

"Why do you keep your money in the refrigerator?"
"I want to have cold cash handy."

"I heard that Jack quit school for a job."
"That's right. Isn't it awful what some people will do for money?"

"What would you do if you had all the money in the world?"
"Pay my wife's bills, as far as it would go."

"How much money do you have in the bank?"
"I don't know. I haven't shaken it lately."

"Why do you look so depressed?"
"Oh, my doctor told me I was as sound as a dollar."

"You couldn't lend me a dollar, could you?"
"No, but I'm going to give you a dime for reading my mind correctly."

"What? Another dress? Where will I get the money to pay for it?"
"But darling, you know I'm not nosey."

"If I had a million dollars, do you know where I would be right now?"
"I know. You'd be on our honeymoon."

"I feel like two cents."
"Well, everything is higher these days."

"Lend me five for a week, old dear?"
"Who's the weak old dear?"

"Can you lend me a tenner for a month, old boy?"
"What does a month-old boy want with a tenner?"

"Say, do you have enough confidence to lend me a dollar?"
"I have the confidence but I don't have the dollar."

The Moon

Girls who have already tried everything under the sun to land a husband should try it under the moon.

The man in the moon was never as interesting as a girl in the sun.

The moon not only pulls the ocean back and forth in the tides, it stops cars on the sides of the roads.

Mothers-In-Law

Be kind to your mother-in-law. Babysitters are expensive!

The penalty for bigamy is having two mothers-in-law.

Divorce is the best way of getting rid of a mother-in-law.

As welcome as a mother-in-law on a honeymoon.

As cold as a mother-in-law's kiss.

Surplus: something you have no need for, like a mother-in-law.

Mixed emotion: Watching your mother-in-law drive off a cliff in your new car.

They now have a mother-in-law sandwich: cold shoulder with salty tongue.

They say every woman has her price. I've got a mother-in-law I can let you have cheap.

Sometimes you can't tell if a man is trying so hard to be a success to please his wife or to spite his mother-in-law.

He who falls in love with himself has no mother-in-law.

No man is really successful until his mother-in-law admits it.

I like Thanksgiving. It's the only time and day I can give my mother-in-law the bird.

Mothers-in-law are not so bad after all; in fact, most of them are fair to meddling.

I hate my mother-in-law. Of course, I know without her I wouldn't have my wife. And that's another reason I hate her.

When they asked me to donate something for the old-age home, I offered them my mother-in-law.

I had the 24-hour virus — a visit from my mother-in-law.

We had a blessed event at our house — my mother-in-law finally left.

A mother-in-law should be careful not to go too far, unless she stays there.

I'd like to smother my mother-in-law in diamonds — but there must be a cheaper way.

Adam was the luckiest man in the world. No mother-in-law.

I just got back from a pleasure trip. Took my mother-in-law to the station.

My car has had stereo for a long time. My wife in front and my mother-in-law in the back.

I told my wife many times: "I like your mother-in-law better than mine!"

Only Adam had no mother-in-law. That's how we know he lived in paradise.

Think you've got troubles? My mother-in-law has a twin sister.

I wouldn't complain that my mother-in-law visits us twice a year. But does she have to stay six months every time?

"Your mother-in-law visited you only once?"
"Yes, she came the day we were married and never left."

"I have a surprise for you, dear!"
"Oh, how long is your mother going to stay with us this time?"

"I heard your mother-in-law was dangerously ill last week."
"Yes, but this week she is dangerously well again."

"Yesterday while hunting you almost shot my mother-in-law."
"Sorry, here's my gun. Have a shot at mine."

"I'm sorry to hear that your mother-in-law died. What was the complaint?"
"I haven't heard any, so far."

Moths

A moth is an animal that can eat a modern bathing suit in one gulp.

A moth is an animal that spends the summer in fur coats and the winter in bathing suits.

These mothballs are hard to use. I threw a whole box of them and didn't hit a single moth.

Mama moth to baby moth: "If you don't eat up all your gabardine you won't get any crepe de chine!"

Camphor is the only thing moths don't give a damphor.

MOTH: A small insect that's always in the hole.

"I choose my clothes."
"That's funny. I've got moths that chew mine."

"What animal eats the least?"
"A moth. It just eats holes."

Mouths

He only opens his mouth when he has nothing to say.

She has lips like cherries and a nose to match.

She never wears any lipstick. She can't keep her mouth still long enough to put it on.

Every time I open my mouth my wife interrupts.

I would buy her some lipstick but I don't know the size of her mouth.

Her mouth is so small, she uses a shoe horn to take an aspirin.

Their marriage is an open and shut proposition. Every time he opens his mouth, she shuts it.

To avoid trouble we should always breathe through the nose. That way we will keep our mouths shut.

My wife will never learn how to swim. She couldn't keep her mouth shut that long.

A yawn is nature's way of letting a married man open his mouth.

She not only has a big mouth she also has a big appetite.

Her picture has to be taken with a fast camera if you want to catch her with her mouth closed.

There is only one trouble with lipstick: it doesn't.

The best way to keep lipstick from smearing is to eat a lot of garlic.

The best way to get some people to agree with you is to keep your mouth shut.

A mouth is another thing that is often opened by mistake.

She gets so tired she can hardly keep her mouth open.

I like a girl to wear lipstick. I've got to have a target.

She has a mouth like a mailbox — open day and night.

She is so tight-lipped, a tube of lipstick lasts her for five years.

"Should teenagers wear lipstick?"
"Only girl teenagers."

"I don't think success has gone to her head."
"No, just to her mouth."

"When you yawn, put your hand in front of your mouth."
"What? And get bitten?"

Movies

Old movies never die. They are just being shown at the late, late show.

He took some cream and sugar to the movies when he heard they were going to have a serial.

He goes to the drive-in with a rented double-decker bus. He likes to sit in the balcony.

I went to a sneak-preview and I was glad they let me sneak out.

This picture is so sad, during intermission they sell candy, popcorn and Kleenex.

During the preview of this film everybody had a good time, except the audience.

I watched a love-scene at a drive-in movie for a whole hour before I realized I was facing the wrong way.

She's the kind of girl you take to the movie when you want to see the picture.

The best way to enjoy a picture is to send your girls' parents to the movie.

I saw Bob Hope's latest picture and I almost died. Some popcorn stuck in my throat.

The picture was so bad we had to sit through it four times to get our money's worth.

I took my girl to the movie last night. We couldn't get seats in the balcony so we had to watch the picture.

Even the French are now making unusual movies. I saw one in which the boy and girl were married.

Old folks tell the darndest tales. Grandfather claims that in his day you had to go to a movie to see a picture.

One thing about old TV movies, they'll never turn out as many as I can turn off.

M-G-M kept calling me, but I wouldn't answer. I didn't like what they called me.

I saw a movie last night with a surprise ending. It was over in 90 minutes, instead of three hours.

I went to a wonderful movie. So refreshing — I felt like a new man when I woke up.

"I'm well-known. You must have seen me in the movies."
"Where do you usually sit?"

"Don't you hate people who talk behind your back?"
"Yes, especially at the movies."

"How did you enjoy the movie?"
"It was awful. I could hardly sit through it a second time."

"Why do you keep buying tickets? You only need one."
"I know, but this man at the entrance keeps tearing them up!"

"Why did you put a TV set in your garage?"
"Now we can go to our own drive-in movie."

Music

He broke his drum just to look inside and see what makes all that noise.

He put his radio into the refrigerator to get some cool music.

His brother broke one of the strings in his guitar and won't tell him which one.

He tied his hands so he could play the piano by ear.

Music isn't always as bad as it sounds.

Modern music is the kind that is played so fast you can't tell what classical composer it was stolen from.

"I play by ear."
"I listen the same way."

"I feel fit as a fiddle."
"But you look like a saxophone."

"How do you get to Carnegie Hall?"
"Practice, man, practice!"

"Will you please open the piano?"
"I can't. The keys are inside."

"What do you think of my orchestra?"
"So you're wondering too?"

"I heard you are a musician?"
"No, but I play the saxophone."

"Why do you keep your violin in the icebox?"
"I like to play it cool!"

"Can you play the piano?"
"I don't know. I never tried."

"I am a finished pianist."
"I know. As a pianist you are finished."

"Where is your young brother?"
"He's in the house playing a piano duet. I finished first."

"Isn't he rather young to be leading the orchestra?"
"Not the way he leads it."

"Why did you put your saxophone up for sale?"
"I saw my neighbor coming home with a gun."

"Do you play piano by ear?"
"No, I play it by the window to annoy the neighbors."

"Do you like Chopin?"
"No, I'm getting tired walking from store to store."

N

Names

She calls me Bias. Buy us this and buy us that.

He told his mother he was glad she named him Bill because everybody calls him by that name.

My wife calls me "Darling" twice a year. Before her birthday and before Christmas.

There is a man who had such a long name, he spoiled a dozen pens in signing one check.

"Are you chewing gum?"
"No, I'm John Smith."

"What's the name of your parents?"
"Mama and papa."

"I love men who are frank."
"Too bad, my name is Joe."

"What's the name of your new baby brother?"
"I don't know. I can't understand a word he says."

"What do you call a man who lends his tools to a neighbor?"
"A saw loser."

"Are you hurt? Give me your name so we can notify your family."
"My family knows my name."

"Does this letter belong to you? The name is obliterated."
"Can't be. My name is Smith."

"You never heard of the Ten Commandments? What's your name?"
"Moses."

"Hey, Noah, wanna drink?"
"Noah don't!"

"Say, who are you shoving?"
"I dunno. What's your name?"

"What would you call a person who would eat his mother's sister?"
"I guess an aunt-eater!"

"Please, call me a taxi."
"Okay, you're a taxi, but you look more like a truck to me."

"Say, aren't you hot from the sun?"
"No, I'm Smith from the Times."

Necks

She has a neck like a swan. Too bad it isn't as white.

I've been kissing her on the neck but I won't anymore. My teeth get caught in her wrinkles.

The only thing that has a neck but no head is a bottle.

A neck is something which, if you don't stick it out, you won't get into trouble up to.

I call my girl "Laryngitis" because she's a pain in the neck.

I thought she was a clean girl until I saw her neck.

A hole is nothing at all, but you can break your neck in it.

Neighbors

I don't have to tell my wife anything. My neighbors do it for me.

The best way to meet a new neighbor is to play your TV set too loud at 2 a.m.

The best way to love your neighbor is when her husband is out of town.

I have a very bad neighbor. He keeps borrowing back everything I take from him.

Love thy neighbor. You'll never know when your TV set is going to be out of order.

It is hard to keep up with the neighbors without falling behind with the creditors.

My neighbors are keeping me broke. They are always buying things I can't afford.

Summer must be over. My neighbor just returned my lawn furniture.

Neighbors are people who wonder when your loud party will end.

A neighbor is a person who will borrow your pot and then cook your goose.

A neighbor is a person who listens to your conversation through a wall.

A good neighbor is a person who can watch you take it easy without thinking you're just lazy.

A good neighbor is a person who, when he wants to borrow a corkscrew, asks you to bring it over.

Newspapers

What a newspaper man he is. Yesterday he came in with two scoops — one chocolate and one vanilla.

"Excuse me sir, are you reading the paper you're sitting on?"

I used to be an old newspaper man. But I had to give it up. I couldn't make any money selling old newspapers.

He used to be a newspaper reporter. He reported how many papers were left on the stands each night.

There's never anything new in the newspapers. All the same things are happening only to different people.

A good way to get your name in the newspapers is to walk across the street reading one.

"My rich uncle owns a newspaper."
"So what? A paper is only ten cents."

"Why do you walk two miles every morning?"
"I'm a newspaper man and I try to keep up my circulation."

New Year's Eve

What a party. The New Year came in and I went out.

The only thing she gives up for Lent is her New Year's resolution.

New Year's Eve is the only time of the year you blow your horn instead of your top.

A New Year's resolution is something that goes in one year and out the other.

The only thing more depressing than staying home on New Year's Eve is going out.

For this New Year's Eve party I won't need any noise-makers. I'm taking my wife along.

Night Clubs

A night club is . . .

. . . a place where people go to eat, drink and be mentioned.

. . . a place where people with nothing to remember go to forget.

. . . a place where you pay a fancy figure for checking your hat.

. . . a place where people go who are not hungry, to eat things they don't like, at prices they can't afford.

. . . a place where the cover charge covers nothing.

I wouldn't say this place was crowded, but they had more waiters than customers.

This place is so expensive, I took one look at the prices on the menu and lost my appetite.

This place is so high class, you pick up the check with the fork.

What a fancy place! Before you use the fingerbowl you have to wash your hands.

This place is so exclusive, *nobody's* allowed in!

Was that place crowded! I scratched my leg and two girls screamed.

A drink in the hand is worth two dollars in a night club.

It was so crowded when I scratched my back the other fellow said: "AHHH!"

This place was so crowded even the waiters were standing.

This place was so expensive, I couldn't even afford the tip.

No wonder nobody comes here. It's always so crowded!

Business was so bad, the waiters were dancing with the chairs.

Everything is done in style here. They have midgets serving the shrimp cocktails.

They keep the lights very low, so you can't see the prices on the menu.

Business was so bad the doorman got arrested for loitering.

I'm always trying to find a nightclub where the checks are as small as the tables.

This nightclub was so crowded I was dancing with the girl behind me, cheek to cheek.

"Thanks for showing me the night club, Bill. Maybe next time we'll go in!"

Here they've got the nicest table I was ever under.

He usually takes his wife to a night club. It's the only place still open by the time she gets dressed.

The night club business has been so bad, when you phone for reservations, they ask you what time you want the show to go on.

"Was it crowded at the night club last night?"
"Not under my table."

"Why did the man cut a hole in the rug?"
"He wanted to see the floor show."

Noses

Big noses usually run in some families.

"Is that your nose or are you eating a banana?"

A powdered nose is no guarantee of a clean neck.

You've heard of nose drops? Hers did.

The best way to avoid a nose bleed is to keep out of other people's business.

An itch is something that when both hands are full your nose always.

It makes a big difference whether glasses are used under or over the nose.

We call our child "Nose" because he's always running.

His nose is so big, while walking in France he caught a cold in England.

He is the only guy who wears sunglasses to protect his eyes from the glare of his nose.

A handkerchief manufacturer is a man who loves to have people sticking their noses in his business.

A specialist told me that to avoid trouble, I should breathe through the nose. That way I will keep my mouth shut.

Then he kissed me and I knew it was puppy love. His nose was cold.

I wanted to buy her some handkerchiefs but I didn't know the size of her nose.

Don't follow your nose, even if it is running.

There's a Russian singer who sings through his nose. He's afraid to open his mouth.

Nudism

He was thrown out of the nudist camp because he had a coat on his tongue.

I could never be a nudist. I always spill hot coffee in my lap.

I can't blame him for being a nudist. He was born that way.

She is a very strict nudist. Won't even use dressing on her salad.

He was asked to grow a beard so he could go to the village for supplies.

I took my girl to a nudist camp and nothing looked good on her.

Where does a nudist put his keys after he locks his car?

When a nudist couple gets a divorce, it's usually because they have been seeing too much of each other.

They have special cards now for nudists: An Airy Christmas and a Happy Nude Year!

There *is* one advantage to being a nudist: you don't have to sit around in a wet bathing suit.

A nudist never has to hold out his hand to see if it is raining.

What a nudist camp. They wouldn't let people in with tattoos. Claimed the pictures spoiled the view.

Did you hear about the nudist who kept feeling hot and cold all over?

"Are they men or women?"
"I can't tell. They have no clothes on."

"Why did you join the nudist colony?"
"Well, my wife wears my pants, my son uses my suits and the tax office took the shirt off my back."

Nurses

A practical nurse is one who married a rich patient.

A nurse is a girl who holds your hand and expects your temperature to go down.

After two days in the hospital, I took a turn for the nurse.

We call the nurse "Tonsil" because so many doctors took her out.

I asked one nurse for a bedpan but she wouldn't give it to me. She said she was the head nurse.

Then I complained because the nurse kept giving me nuts when I kept asking her for dates.

Her, a nurse? She couldn't put a dressing on a salad!

O

Opera

The trouble with opera is that there's too much singing

I go to the opera whether I need the sleep or not.

Opera in English is a fine idea. It helps you understand what's boring you.

I go to the opera every season. I like to see how the other half sleeps.

Our family has more trouble than a soap opera.

An opera singer is a singer who is always telling his troubles.

An opera is a place where a guy gets stabbed in the back and, instead of bleeding, he sings.

The Beggar's Opera, written by John Gay and produced by John Rich, was said to have made Rich gay and Gay rich.

If you get to the opera before it's finished, you're on time.

An opera is a place where anything that is too dumb to be spoken is sung.

A soap opera is corn on the sob.

"What opera experience did you say you had? Horse or soap?"

"Can you hear her singing?"
"No, these are good seats."

"What did Juliet say when she met Romeo in the balcony?"
"Couldn't you get seats in the orchestra?"

"What did you hear in the opera last night?"
"All sort of news. Mrs. Brown dyed her hair, the Smiths are getting a divorce and the Whites are bankrupt."

Operations

Now you need two anesthetics for your operation. One to put you to sleep, and another when you see the bill.

My doctor is so expensive! He operated on me and charged me $300 for new parts.

A monolog is a conversation between a woman who has just had an operation and one who hasn't.

"I'm afraid I can't afford that operation right now."
"No? It looks like you'll have to talk about the old one for another year."

"Did you recover from your operation?"
"Not yet. The doctor says I still have two more payments."

"Did your wife recover from her operation?"
"Not yet. She is still talking about it."

"Tell me, why do doctors wear those masks at operations?"
"That's if something goes wrong, nobody can identify them."

"Could you pay for an operation if I thought one was necessary?"
"Would you find it necessary, Doc, if I couldn't pay for it?"

"So the operation on this man was just in the nick of time."
"Yes, in another ten hours he would have recovered."

Opinions

My wife is the most wonderful woman in the world, and that's not just my opinion — it's hers.

"Listen, you, when I want your opinion I'll give it to you!"

An opinion is something you have on your mind and want to get off your chest.

"I know I'm not good looking. But what's my opinion against thousands of others?"

"Don't you and your wife ever have different opinions?"
"Sure, but I don't tell her about them."

"Do you think I'm a fool?"
"No, but what's my opinion against thousands of others."

Opportunity

The trouble with opportunity is that it always looks bigger coming than going.

Opportunity knocked on my door today but I didn't answer. I waited for him to knock twice.

There are two doors to opportunity: push and pull!

Even when opportunity knocks, a man must get off his seat to open the door.

Opportunity knocked last night and spoiled my opportunity!

Opportunity knocks only once but temptation bangs on the door for years.

When opportunity knocked he complained about the noise.

When opportunity knocks at the door, most people are out in the back yard looking for four-leaf clovers.

Opportunity knocks once and the neighbors the rest of the time.

The husband who talks in his sleep may just be taking advantage of his opportunity.

Oysters

An oyster is a fish that's built like a nut.

The oyster is very unfortunate. It's always getting into a stew.

There is nothing moyster than an oyster in the cloyster.

P

Parties

"But if this isn't a costume party, why do you want me to put a sack over my head?"

It was a Gay-90's party. The men were all gay and the women 90.

I know I had a good time at that party. I was sick for three days.

I believe in the two-party system. One on Friday and one on Saturday.

She had a coming-out party, but they made her go back in again.

My wife even gives me a going-away party when I take out the garbage.

What a party we had. The water was flowing like champagne.

A man can always tell what kind of time he's had at a party by the look on his wife's face.

He was such a bore that people used to have parties just not to have him.

They even gave away door prizes. One fellow won six doors.

You always can tell the host at the party. He's the one who is watching the clock.

Don't try to make your guests feel at home. If they wanted to feel at home, they would have stayed there.

Then there was the woman with varicose veins who went to the masquerade party as a road map.

I didn't want to go empty handed, so I wore gloves.

My dog was the life of the party; that gives you an idea of how dull it was.

"We hate to eat and run – but I'm still hungry!"

Going to a party with your wife is like going fishing with the game warden.

It was a novelty party. Every man brought his own wife.

I know a couple who are always the life of the party, but it is not always the same party.

I went to a surprise party. I was surprised when they let me in.

Socially, she's the creme de la crumb.

The fellow who didn't want to come to the party is usually the one who doesn't want to go home.

Too much celebrating has kept many a man from becoming celebrated.

"Your friend Joe seemed to be the life of the party."
"Yes, he was the only one who could talk louder than the TV."

"Didn't you hear me pounding on the ceiling?"
"Oh, that's all right. We were making a lot of noise ourselves."

"Did you go to Bertie's party?"
"No, the invitation said from four to nine, and I'm ten."

"Wonderful party, isn't it?"
"Yes, who is giving it?"

"How was the party last night?"
"Oh, the party was nice, so we left and went to my apartment."

"Their parties are always so formal and stiff."
"That's right. She is so formal and he gets so stiff."

"Did you have a nice time at the party?"
"So they tell me."

People

The only thing some people pay is attention.

The only time some people have more money than brains is on payday.

It takes three kinds of people to make the world: right-handed, left-handed and underhanded.

It is easy to see through people who make spectacles of themselves.

There are now three classes of people: the haves, the have-nots, and the charge-its.

Have you noticed that single people aren't married?

I hear he is from Baltimore. Sort of a Baltimoron.

The trouble with most people is their trouble.

We had nothing in common. She was a girl and I was a man.

Sometimes I feel like resigning from the human race – if I only knew where to send my resignation.

A skeleton is nothing but a stack of bones with the people scraped off.

Here is a fellow who's knock-kneed, cross-eyed, overweight and stupid – and those are his good points.

I'm known as a Minute Man. When I say something I minute.

When everybody is somebody, then nobody is anybody.

There are two kinds of people: those in the swim and those in the soup.

"Will you join me?"
"Why, are you coming apart?"

"You look pretty sad."
"That's why I'm looking sad!"

"I'm not myself tonight."
"Yes, I've noticed the improvement."

"Do you ever think of me?"
"Yes, but I hate to tell you what."

"These people knew me when I was only a bum."
"You haven't changed a bit."

"He is really a good kid when you get to know him."
"But who wants to know him?"

"I'm nobody's fool!"
"Well, maybe you can get somebody to adopt you?"

"I'm looking for the people who live here."
"Well, you came to the right place."

"But I'm telling you I'm not Charlie."
"I thought so! You don't even resemble him."

"You are a low-down, ignorant, worthless person."
"Well, nobody is perfect!"

"What did one ghost say to the other?"
"Do you believe in people?"

"I met a man just now I haven't seen in 20 years."
"That's nothing. I met a man just now I never saw before in my life."

Perfume

. . . A pretty gift that costs a man a pretty scent.

. . . Any smell that is used to drown a worse one.

. . . A sweet odor that holds you smellbound.

She calls her perfume "Trapeze" because there's danger in every drop.

She bought some perfume called "High Heaven" and it certainly smelled to that.

They now have a new perfume that drives women crazy. It smells like money.

Photography

Our family is so ugly, we keep the negatives in our family album.

I used to be twins. My mother has a picture of me when I was two.

This is a wedding picture of my parents. The little fellow in between is me.

I was a beautiful child. My parents used to have me kidnaped just to see my picture in the papers.

She reminds me of a roll of film: undeveloped.

If you really look like your passport photo, chances are you're not well enough to travel.

She looks even worse than her passport photo.

There are now so many tourists they are getting in each other's snapshots.

On those passport pictures, most people look as if they needed the trip.

On vacation, people drive thousands of miles to have their picture taken in front of their cars.

"Look pleasant, please. As soon as I snap the picture, you can resume your natural expression."

"Honey, what kind of pictures have you been taking that you have to develop them in the dark?"

As lightning flashed across the window, little Bobbie said: "Smile everybody. God is taking our picture!"

A photo of a girl in a bikini is not a snapshot — it's an exposure!

"It must be hard to take a picture."
"Not at all. It's a snap!"

"I don't like this photo. It doesn't do me justice."
"It's mercy you want, not justice."

"Sure, we make life-size enlargements."
"Good. Here is a picture of an elephant."

"What has to be taken before you get it?"
"A photograph."

"Doc, I'm worried. My little son swallowed the film out of my camera."
"Don't worry. Nothing will develop."

"What is there that you cannot take with a camera?"
"A hint."

"Have you had any luck with your camera?"
"Oh, I took a picture that a man paid me $100 to destroy."

Pickpockets

There is a three-fingered pickpocket who only steals bowling balls.

If a pickpocket would go through my pockets now, all he would get is exercise.

Old pickpockets never die, they just steal away!

The best way to bring money home from the race track is to be a pickpocket.

Police

He wanted to sleep in the open air; that's why he wanted to join the police force.

Did you hear about the cop who gave out 24 parking tickets before he discovered he was in a drive-in-movie?

My uncle is now with the F.B.I. They finally caught up with him.

Cop to girl: "I only want your name and address. I'm not interested in your phone number!"

This policeman found a stolen car on Porphyry Street, and right away he pushed the car to Park Street. He couldn't spell Porphyry.

"Officer, where do I go to apologize for shooting my husband?"

Policeman to Motorist: "I'd give you a ticket for parking if I could find a place to park my motorcycle."

He is sure a bad detective. I'm sure he would have trouble finding an elephant with a nosebleed in the snow.

A policeman wanted to give me a ticket because I hit him. Why did he stand in the middle of the street?

"Pull over. O.K., now where is the fire?"
"In your eyes, officer, in your eyes!"

Politics

The man who goes into politics as a business has no business going into politics.

I know a politician who is so old, he doesn't run for office — he walks.

I made so much money betting on the Democrats I became a Republican.

I voted five times but they can't bother me. I'm not a citizen.

The trouble with the politicians today is that they take the floor only to hit the ceiling.

Anybody who says he understands international affairs these days is two weeks behind the news.

This politician has announced that he perfectly understands the questions of the day. The trouble is he doesn't know the answers.

Both candidates are ready and willing. Now if we could only find one who's able.

The polls are places where you stand in line for a chance to decide who will spend your money.

Congress is shrewd. First they put a big tax on liquor. Then they raise all other taxes to drive people to drink.

Popularity

To be popular a girl must do the wrong thing at the right time.

I was so popular in school, everybody hated me.

She is so unpopular her phone doesn't even ring when she's in the shower.

The Post Office

The new clerk at the Post Office is so dumb, he tried to put a zip code number on Lincoln's Gettysburg Address.

I ordered a vacuum cleaner by mail, but I couldn't get it out of the mailbox.

Have you noticed that it now takes six cents for you to say your two-cents worth on a penny post card?

If the world is getting smaller, why do they raise the postal rates?

A postman is a man from whom all the girls get love letters.

An eccentric person is a person who pays more for used stamps than for new ones.

Old postmen never die. They just lose their zip.

Today's president is tomorrow's five cent stamp.

No postage stamp sticks better than the one on an envelope with the wrong address.

She invited me to come and play post office, but I forgot her zip code.

Every time I pass our post office I notice a terrible smell. That must come from the dead letters.

A small-town post office returned a letter with this remark: Addressee died a year ago. Left no forwarding address.

If postal rates go up again we may have a rates riot.

He had a job at the post office, but he was fired. Every time someone handed him a package he would ask: "Oh, for me?"

"How can you keep postage stamps from sticking together?"
"Buy them one at a time!"

"How much does a two-cent stamp cost?"
"What size?"

"Shall I put the stamp on myself?"
"No, on the letter."

"Madam, you put too much postage on this letter."
"Oh, Heavens, I hope it won't go too far now."

"This letter is too heavy; you have to put more stamps on."
"That will make it lighter?"

"What can go all around the world and still stay in one corner?"
"A postage stamp."

"Can you spell a word that has more than 100 letters in it?"
"Post Office."

Poverty

There's one good thing about being poor — it's inexpensive.

The easiest way to remain poor is to pretend to be rich.

It's no disgrace to be poor but it's mighty inconvenient.

Blessed are the poor. The more things you can afford, the more things you have to dust.

I was too poor to take treatments from my doctor, so for a small fee he touched up my X-Rays.

My parents could never afford to buy me shoes, so they painted my feet black and laced up my toes.

There's one thing money can't buy: poverty!

Being poor has one distinct advantage. It doesn't take much to improve your situation.

We were so poor, whenever I got alphabet soup I only found one letter in it.

In the old days we were so poor we *had* to eat hamburgers. Now we're poor *because* we eat hamburgers.

He was so poor . . .

. . . he bought a little piggy bank and then had no money left to put in it.

. . . he bought only one shoe at a time.

. . . he could afford only to play golf once a month.

. . . he could have only one measle at a time.

. . . he had to wash his Cadillac himself.

. . . he had to watch TV by candlelight.

. . . he used old newspapers for wall-to-wall carpeting.

. . . he walked twice a week to the opera to save car fare.

. . . he was 14 when he found out that people eat three meals a day.

Psychiatrists

The auto mechanic went to the psychiatrist and laid down under the couch.

This cannibal went to a psychiatrist because he was fed up with people.

I don't go to my psychiatrist any more. He was meddling too much in my private life.

There is nothing wrong with the average person that a good psychiatrist can't exaggerate.

She refused to see a psychiatrist because she doesn't trust any man who keeps a couch in his office.

He charged him a double fee because he had a split personality.

When you show some improvement he lets you sit up on the couch.

My psychiatrist is great. He lumped all my nagging little worries into one big complex.

I've been going to a psychiatrist for years, and I just found out he's been deaf since birth.

Latest thing in group therapy: instead of couches they use bunk beds.

My psychiatrist cures alcoholism. He charges so much you can't afford to buy liquor.

It's easy to spot a psychiatrist in a nudist camp. He's the one who's listening instead of looking.

"Thanks for curing me of gambling, doctor. Now give me your bill and I'll toss you double or nothing for it."

She's so homely the psychiatrist asked her to lie face down on the coach.

Three out of five people go to psychiatrists. The other two are psychiatrists.

My psychiatrist is so busy he has an upper and lower berth.

Show me a psychiatrist and I'll show you a couch coach.

My psychiatrist is so poor he can't afford a couch. He uses a cot.

He is a friendly psychiatrist. He lies down on the couch with you.

In Hollywood if you don't have a psychiatrist, people think you're crazy.

My psychiatrist is so poor, whenever he gets a patient he has to run out and rent a couch.

Any man who goes to a psychiatrist should have his head examined.

He's a fine psychiatrist. Eight visits and he cured me of $250.

He is doing so well, he has had his couch reupholstered four times.

My psychiatrist is so strict, he gives me homework. I have to go straight home and dream.

This psychiatrist sure cures people by shock treatment. He bills them in advance.

But he helped me a lot. I would never answer the phone, because I was afraid. Now I answer it whether it rings or not.

Just because a man asks you to lie down on a couch doesn't mean he's a psychiatrist.

My wife's visit to the psychiatrist was a waste of time. She spent the first 40 minutes rearranging the couch.

My girl visited the psychiatrist, but he couldn't get her to start talking until he put a phone in her hand.

This poor psychiatrist hasn't got a couch — just sleeping bags.

You ought to meet my psychiatrist. He's wonderful. He always finds something wrong with you.

This psychiatrist had an electric vibrator installed in his couch and picked up a fortune in loose change.

A psychiatrist's couch is where you land when you go off your rocker.

"Imagine meeting you here at the psychiatrist's office. Are you coming or going?"
"If I knew that, I wouldn't be here!"

"Doctor, every day when I come home from work my wife throws dishes at me, never cooks for me and always calls me awful names."
"That's an easy case. I think she doesn't like you."

R

Radios

"Time out for a record and then back to our commercials."

"Tune in again, next week: same station, same time, same jokes!"

"And now for the news that happened during the commercials."

"And now we bring you an unimportant announcement from our sponsor."

"When you hear the gong will someone please phone in the correct time. Our clock stopped!"

The only thing we get on our radio is dust!

I'm working on something new: color radio.

I just invented a new kind of television. It's called radio!

I have a two-way radio. It either plays or it doesn't.

Now they have frozen radio dinners — for people who don't own a TV set.

Nowadays you have to be a success on radio before you can become a failure on television.

I wouldn't say she's ugly, but she has a perfect face for radio.

She kept playing two transistor radios next to her ears and wound up with a stereophonic headache.

"And now a word from our sponsor, who made this program impossible."

A radio announcer is a man who talks until you have a headache, and then tries to sell you a remedy for it.

A radio announcer is a person who works for the love of mike.

A fellow said he liked his radio better than his wife because he gets less interference from it.

The longest word in the English language is the one following the phrase: "And now, just a word from our announcer about a fine product."

He just installed a new loud speaker in his house. He got married again.

"This is a radio survey. To whom are you listening?"
"My wife."

"I just bought a Japanese radio."
"But how can you understand the language?"

"I'll turn on the radio if you're a music lover."
"Oh, I can love with or without music."

"On my radio I can get Boston and Denver."
"That's nothing. I stick my head out the window and get chilly."

"Can you play a musical instrument?"
"No, I can't even play a radio."

"What keeps going and going but is never gone?"
"A radio."

Railroads

"Hello, Grand Central? Do you have a sleeping car? You do? Well, wake it up!"

"For gosh sakes, conductor, let me off at the next stop. I thought this was a lunch wagon!"

Science is resourceful. They couldn't pry open the Pullman windows, so they air-conditioned the trains.

My brother is a haberdasher for the railroad. He is in charge of the ties.

The world's worst train robbery is what they charge for a hamburger in the dining car.

"Never the twain shall meet!" said the little boy as the brakeman threw the switch.

Don't race trains to crossings. If it is a tie, you lose.

The town was so small, when the train stopped at the station, the engine was way out in the country.

For Christmas I bought my son a set of electric trains for me to play with.

A certain railroad, to speed up service, now puts the stations closer together.

Every time I reach the station I miss my train.

The best way to miss the train is at a crossing.

I call my girl "Third Rail" because every time I touch her I get shocked.

He kept on chewing gum on the train because the engine said: "Choo-choo!"

"Are you an uptown train?"
"No, I'm a conductor!"

"How can you tell when a train is gone?"
"It leaves its tracks behind."

"Does this train stop at Grand Central?"
"If it doesn't there will be a big crash."

"Is this train on time?"
"We're satisfied if it is on the track."

"Why did they build the station so far out of town?"
"They wanted to have it near the tracks."

"Say, conductor, the train is running smoother now."
"Yes, we are off the track now."

"Which end of the train should I get off?"
"Either one. It stops at both ends."

"Have you a ladies' waiting room in this station?"
"No, madam, but we have a room for ladies who can't wait."

"You haven't got on enough clothes to flag a train."
"Who wants to flag a train?"

"It is disgusting the way those men are staring at the girl getting on the train."
"What train?"

"This train goes to Buffalo and points East."
"I want a train that goes to Syracuse and I don't care which way it points."

"I want a ticket around the world?"
"One way?"

"I want to catch a late train to New York."
"Take the 6:45. That's usually as late as any."

"I'm sorry, Madam, but your ticket is for New York and this train is going to Chicago."
"My goodness, conductor, does the engineer know he's going the wrong way?"

Rain

I can't understand why it's still raining. The weekend is over.

We really don't need any calendars. When it rains it's Sunday.

I can make it rain any time I want to. All I have to do is wash my car.

I can tell if it's raining by my corns. If they get wet, it's raining.

The only good thing about rain is that you don't have to shovel it!

Into each life some rain must fall — usually on weekends.

Every time I wear my spring coat in the rain the springs get rusty.

Rubbers are something that if your feet are dry you haven't walked in the rain without.

An hour of rain will do more good in five minutes than a month of it would do in a week.

Rain is something that makes flowers grow and taxicabs disappear.

Everybody enjoys walking in the rain except the people who have to.

They now have a picnic doll: you wind it up and it rains.

My wife is very neat. When it rains we have wall-to-wall newspapers.

"Do you think it will rain?"
"It all depends on the weather."

"Is it raining outside?"
"Did it ever rain inside?"

"Did you save anything for a rainy day?"
"Yes, the washing of my car."

"Did you put anything away for a rainy day?"
"Yes, two pair of galoshes."

"Your beard is on fire!"
"I know. Can't you see I'm praying for rain?"

"It's raining cats and dogs outside."
"I know. I just stepped into a poodle."

"Did it rain last night! You never saw such a storm."
"Why didn't you wake me? You know I can't sleep during a storm."

"It's raining, let's hurry."
"If we hurry will it rain less?"

Reno

... A place where people go to kick the marriage habit.

... A place where the cream of the crop goes through the separator.

... A place where Declarations of Independence are signed.

... The great divide.

... The land of the free and the grave of the home.

... The last mile of the wedding march.

... The original separation center.

... The residence of the bitter half.

... Sue City.

Restaurants

I ordered a hot chocolate and the waiter brought me a Hershey chocolate bar and a match.

They serve instant food here. You get sick the instant you eat it.

I always take her to the finest restaurants. Someday I'll take her inside.

Well, here it is April. I hope they will change the tablecloth now!

This is a combination restaurant and filling station. You can get food here and gas.

The food was so bad I wanted to complain to the manager, but I didn't want to stay in line.

My favorite restaurant hires only married men. They are used to taking orders.

What a restaurant! It's one of those places where if you don't smell it, they haven't got it.

I ordered turkey and even the dark meat looked white. It was cut so thin you could see the plate through it.

This is a fine Chinese restaurant. They serve you all the food you can eat for 50 cents. The trouble is they give you only one chopstick.

In this place, as soon as you sit down they put the food on the table. I wish they would use plates.

When ordering in a fancy restaurant, watch out. If you can't pronounce it, you can't afford it!

Every time I eat in a Chinese restaurant I find the address of the nearest doctor in my fortune cookie.

I always eat doughnuts in this restaurant so I can look through the hole and see if anybody is stealing my hat and coat.

I was in the restaurant business but I had to give it up. The dishes got dirty.

It's a fine restaurant. If you ask for bread they bring it to you – right after dessert.

I wouldn't say this place was expensive, but you need a co-signer for a ham sandwich.

They now have a restaurant where they give you nagging service – for home-sick husbands.

The food in this place is so bad, if it weren't for salt and pepper I'd starve to death.

They have a yo-yo special here – a piece of spaghetti wrapped around a meatball.

This isn't exactly a restaurant. It's more like a Bureau of Missing Portions.

They've got a speciality that melts in your mouth. Ice cream!

It's the kind of restuarant people stay in front of while deciding where to eat.

This is a very high class restaurant. They even make gravy to match your vest.

Monday nights they are closed. That's the day they wash the dishes.

"You say the service is bad here! Wait till you eat the food."

The service here is so slow, you have to come at lunchtime to be served supper.

This new Chinese restaurant is so chic, the menus are printed in French.

Hungry? She ordered everything on the menu but the restâurant's address.

In here they are very considerate. They give you dull knives so you can't cut your lips.

The kitchen here must be very clean. Everything tastes like soap.

The meat is tender here but the check is tough.

I like to eat in places where they have a jukebox. Sometimes the music helps you forget the food and sometimes the food helps to forget the music.

An after-dinner mint is what a man needs nowadays to pay for the restaurant check.

The food here is absolutely poison and such small portions!

Prices in restuarants are now so high it is wiser to watch your steak than your hat and coat.

"Today I have fried liver, boiled tongue, stewed kidneys and pig's feet."
"Don't tell me your ailments, waiter. I came for a steak dinner."

"Waiter, I won't have any more mushrooms today. I was nearly poisoned by them last week."
"Is that so? Then I won the bet with our cook."

"Say, waiter, what's the difference between the one dollar steak and the two dollar steak?"
"The two dollar steak costs exactly one dollar more."

"I eat in a different restaurant every day."
"I don't tip either."

"Is this restaurant a good place to go?"
"It's a good place to go, but a terrible place to eat."

"How do you know this is a real Mexican restaurant?"
"You're not supposed to drink their water."

"How did you ever get into the restaurant business?"
"I walked in to change a $20 bill and they made me a partner."

"The food is terrible here. I'd like to see the manager."
"Sorry, sir. He's out for lunch."

"What do I have to do to get a glass of water in this place?"
"Set yourself on fire, sir."

"There's soap in this food, waiter!"
"That's all right. It's to wash the food down."

"Your menu says Cold Boiled Ham. What is that?"
"That's ham boiled in cold water, sir."

"Waiter, do you have frog's legs?"
"No, sir. Rheumatism makes me walk like this."

"Say, waiter, why do you have your thumb on my steak?"
"I don't want it to fall on the floor again."

"Say, waiter, there's a button in my salad."
"I suppose it fell off while the salad was dressing."

S

Savings

Nowadays, a dollar saved is a quarter earned.

She found a new way to save money: she uses mine!

Prices are rising so fast that a dollar saved is 50 cents lost.

What most people like to save for a rainy day is a taxi!

My wife saves Green Stamps as if they were money and spends money as if it were Green Stamps.

My wife will always find the most expensive way to save money.

She just saved me a lot of money: she married someone else.

All I have been able to save for a rainy day is a pair of dry socks.

Some time ago, when you saved money you were a miser. Nowadays, if you save money you're a wizard.

My wife took the money we were saving for a new car and blew it on a movie.

With too many people, all they have saved up for a rainy day is an old umbrella.

Saving is getting along without what you need, in order to have money for something you can do without.

You save your money for a rainy day and then the government comes and soaks you.

My wife saves all the pay envelopes but none of my pay.

The only thing she has saved for a rainy day is an umbrella and a bottle of cold tablets.

School

I will never learn how to spell. The teacher keeps changing the words.

The boys in my class are so tough, that the teacher played hookey.

I only went to school on the first day, just to find out when our vacation begins.

I don't like to go to school. I can't read or write and they won't let me talk.

Then there was the teacher who didn't have a principle.

In my third year in school I won a special award for playing hookey.

The only thing he ever took up in school was space.

He even flunked recess.

My folks are sending me away to school so they won't have to help me with my homework.

"Here is my report card, daddy, and one of yours I found in the attic."

My son refuses to study history any more. He claims they make it faster than he can learn it.

I was so tough I made the teacher stay after school.

One day I brought an apple for the teacher and she kissed me. The next day I brought her a watermelon.

Our son brought home a note from school. They want to have a written excuse for his presence.

"I don't get the best marks in school, daddy, do you get the best salary at your office?"

He got a —1 on his paper. He not only had the wrong answers, he even mispelled his name.

A Report Card is a poison letter written by a teacher.

Old teachers never die, they just grade away.

A school is a place where children go to catch cold from other children so they can stay home.

"How do you spell Mississippi?"
"River or state?"

"Name three collective nouns."
"Fly-paper, waste-basket, and vacuum-cleaner."

"Did your father help you with this homework?"
"No, I got it wrong all by myself."

"In what battle did General Wolfe cry: "I die happy!'?"
"In his last battle."

"Where was the Declaration of Independence signed?"
"At the bottom."

"Now, class, are there any questions?"
"Yes, where do those words go when you rub them off the blackboard?"

"Explain the manners and customs of the natives of Borneo."
"They have no manners and they wear no costumes."

"If I cut two apples and two pears in ten pieces what will I get?"
"Fruit salad."

"What comes after six?"
"The milk man."

"What is black when clean and white when dirty?"
"A blackboard."

"I didn't see any school in this town."
"You didn't. Don't you see that sign across the street: TEECHIN DON HEER!

"I gotta 'A' in spelling."
"You dope! There isn't any 'A' in spelling."

"How far did you go in school?"
"About three miles."

"I heard you missed school yesterday."
"Not a bit."

"Well, how do you like school?"
"Closed."

Scotchmen

A scotchman was hurt while watching a baseball game, so he sued the teams that were playing. He fell out of a tree.

Then there was the Scotch anarchist who lit a bomb and just hated to let go of it.

It's a sure sign of summer when a Scotchman throws his Christmas tree away.

The difference between a Scotchman and a coconut is that you can get a drink out of a coconut.

The difference between a Scotchman and a canoe: a canoe tips.

A Scotchman is a person whose thrift teaches him to take long steps to save shoe leather, but whose caution advises him to take short steps to avoid ripping his pants.

The wristwatch was invented by a Scotchman who objected to taking anything out of his pocket.

Seasickness

Some people get seasick taking a bubble bath.

I found a new cure for seasickness. It's called: a tight collar.

There's no place like Venice. Where else can you get seasick crossing the street?

Seasick? When I sat in a green chair nobody could see me.

I was so sick I had callouses on my stomach from leaning over the rail.

Did you hear about the seasick man who put glue in his soup to keep it down?

"Man overboard!"
"What luck some people have!"

"I always get seasick the first day out."
"Then why don't you go a day late?"

"Hey, you can't get sick on the deck!"
"No? Just watch me!"

"Shall I bring your dinner on the deck, sir?"
"No, just throw it overboard and save time."

Seasons

My wife was spring cleaning again. My wallet is empty.

Fall is the time of the year when summer's suntan turns to winter's frostbite.

I know Fall is here. I just got my air-conditioner back from the repair shop

I like every season. In winter I like the summer and in summer I like winter.

It's Fall, and the family that rakes together aches together.

Secretaries

My secretary can't type too well, but she can erase 50 words a minute.

My secretary is a very poor speller. She even misspelled "P.S."

My secretary is so fat, I don't know whether to pay her by the week or by the pound.

My secretary is very efficient. She hasn't missed a coffee break in ten years.

My secretary knows how to write shorthand, but it takes her much longer.

My secretary quit. She caught me kissing my wife.

My secretary reminds me of my wife. Every time I whisper something in her ear, she says: "Remember, you have a wife!"

My secretary spells atrociously, but others can't spell at all.

My secretary walked into my office and demanded a salary on next week's advances.

My secretary, when told to take some dictation, asked me: "Where to?"

My secretary works a four-day week, but it takes her six days to do it.

My secretary wrote me a note asking for a raise, but she misspelled three words.

"Boss, today I got in on time, to make up for being out yesterday."

"But, boss, I did try to get here on time, but it makes such a long day."

Her spelling is atrocious and her perfume is nasty, but she makes a great cup of coffee.

"But, boss, my typing isn't so bad if you compare it with my shorthand."

"Of course, boss, I can spell correctly, but I'm not too fanatical about it."

"Yes, you may elect to skip coffee breaks entirely and retire three years early."

Her typing is terrible, her shorthand worse, but she is a great conversation piece.

"Get my broker, Miss Jones."
"Yes, sir. Stock or pawn?"

"Can you take dictation?"
"No, I've never been married."

"How is your typing coming along?"
"Fine, I can now make 20 mistakes a minute."

"How long did you work for your last boss?"
"Until he married me."

"How many words can you type a minute?"
"Big ones or little ones?"

"While I was out, did you take any messages?"
"No, sir, are there any missing?"

"My new secretary spells atrociously."
"She must be pretty good. I can't spell that."

"Your little girl wants to kiss you over the phone."
"Take the message, Miss Jones, and I'll get it from you later."

"Didn't my secretary tell you I'm out. How did you know I was in?"
"Easy. She was working hard."

"You'll have to see my secretary for an appointment."
"I did, but she is booked for two weeks."

"I heard you use the Biblical system on your typewriter. How does it go?"
"Seek and ye shall find!"

"How do you spell inconsequentially?"
"Always wrong."

"Who told you that you can be lazy around the office just because I kissed you last night?"
"My lawyer."

"Sorry, Madam, Mr. Brown has just gone out to lunch with his wife."
"Okay, then just tell him that his secretary called!"

Secrets

. . . As unhappy as a woman with a secret nobody wants to know.

A woman will keep one secret: the secret of her age.

She sure can keep a secret. We were engaged for months before I knew it.

Tell a woman a secret and it is no secret any more.

She will never give away a secret, but she will exchange it for another.

The man who has no secrets from his wife either has no secrets or no wife.

I can keep a secret. It's the people I tell it to who can't.

A woman's idea of keeping a secret is to refuse to say who told it to her.

The secret of a secret is to know when and how to tell it.

A woman can keep a secret until she meets another woman.

"Why, no, I didn't tell anyone yet, I didn't know it was a secret!"

My wife can keep a secret – but only one at a time!

There are two kinds of secrets: one is not worth keeping and the other is too good to keep.

A secret is anything a woman doesn't know.

Secrets are things we give to other people to keep for us.

It's not so hard for a woman to keep a secret as it is for her to keep it a secret that she's keeping a secret.

My wife can keep a secret with telling effects.

"Her engagement is still a secret."
"I know. Everybody tells me that."

"I heard you are secretly married to Alice."
"No, she knows all about it."

"Why do you tell everybody I'm a moron?"
"Oh, I didn't know you wanted to keep it a secret."

"What is too much for one, just right for two, but nothing at all for three?"
"A secret."

"Do you know the secret of real popularity?"
"Yes, honey, but my mother said not to."

Shoes

If the new shoes fit, buy a size smaller.

To make your shoes look smaller, wear smaller feet.

Every time I'm in a rush, my shoelaces break.

The new Italian pointed shoes are very comfortable, if you happen to have one toe.

A woman shopping for a pair of shoes couldn't get a fit, but the clerk had one.

To forget all your other troubles, try wearing a pair of shoes that are a size too small.

My mother could never afford to buy me shoes, so she painted my feet black and laced my toes.

It is time to have your shoes re-soled if, when stepping on a nickel you could tell whether it's head or tail.

Ladies like shoes that are big in the inside and small on the outside.

Even low-heel shoes are very high these days.

The poor little shoe was crying because its mother was a sneaker and its father a loafer.

Ever notice that the shoes you hate most are the ones that last the longest.

If both of your shoes feel uncomfortable, maybe you've got them on the wrong foot.

"What would you do if you were in my shoes?"
"Polish them."

"How much are your ten dollar shoes?"
"About five dollars a foot."

"Now go home and soak your feet in hot water."
"What? And get my shoes wet."

"What size shoes do you want?"
"Four is my size, but I always wear seven because four hurt my toes."

"What should I wear with my green and pink-striped stockings?"
"Hip boots."

"Why don't you scrape some of the mud off your shoes?"
"What shoes?"

Shopping

When my wife says "Bye bye," she means "Buy, Buy!"

I finally got a bargain in a 5 & 10 cent store. I found something that cost less than 50 cents.

Every time my wife goes shopping she comes home with everything but money.

The most expensive vehicle to operate, per mile, is the shopping cart.

Yesterday I went window shopping. That's the only kind of shopping I can afford these days.

My wife has been missing for four days. I don't know whether she's left me or gone shopping.

She always puts on her shopping list: meat, biscuits, snacks, vitamins; and that's just for the dog!

My wife went to the corner market. Bought two corners.

Then she went window shopping. Bought five windows.

My wife just took her shopping cart for a 1000 mile checkup.

When my wife suggests going for a spin she usually has her revolving charge account in mind.

Whatever my wife buys today is usually on sale tomorrow.

My wife spent five hours in one store. Her coat got caught in the elevator.

Nowadays a bargain is anything that's only a little overpriced.

My wife is very punctual. In fact, she buys everything on time.

If you don't know what's up, you haven't been shopping lately.

My wife had a typical shopping day. She came home with an empty wallet, three pages of Trading Stamps and two parking tickets.

I won't say my wife is a big spender, but Macy's opened a branch in our living room.

One store was so crowded, two women were trying on the same girdle.

The way some women shop, you would think they were taking inventory of the store.

My wife is just crazy about Macy's. She spent some of the happiest pages of my checkbook on the third floor.

Why does Christmas always come just when the stores are so crowded?

A counterfeit is something a woman has if she can't reach the bargain counter.

A bargain is something that is reasonably priced that a woman can usually find some use for.

Many people buy on time, but only a few pay that way.

Every time my wife looks at my head she puts melon on her shopping list.

Many a man loses his balance when his wife goes shopping.

She shops like a human dynamo — charges everything.

A luxury item is something that costs three dollars to make, six dollars to buy and nine dollars to repair.

"No, madam, we have none."
"Why do you call this a General Store if you have none?"

"Say, do you take anything off for cash?"
"Sir, this is a store, not a burlesque show."

"I'd like to see something nice in silk stockings."
"You men are all alike."

"I want to go shopping, dear. Is the weather favorable? What does the paper say?"
"Rain, snow, tornados, thunder and lightning."

"Why does a woman say she's been shopping when she hasn't bought anything?"
"Why does a man say he's been fishing when he hasn't caught anything?"

"Sir, could I interest you in a new bathing suit?"
"You sure could, but my wife is at the other counter shopping."

Show Business

This next act really has hidden talents. I just hope some day they'll find them.

I will never forget my first words in the theater: Peanuts! Pop corn!

"Him, a juggler? He couldn't catch a cold in Alaska!"

I held the audience open-mouthed. They all yawned at once!

My fan club can hold a mass meeting in a telephone booth.

She calls herself a straight actress. Her measurements are: 36-36-36.

He's got a lot of funny lines. Too bad they are all in his face!

If you think my act is monotonous, you should see my home life!

What his act hasn't got in entertainment, he makes up in boredom!

This show goes on my best-smeller list!

I saw the show under bad conditions. The curtain was up!

The show was full of surprises. I just wish it was full of talents.

This ventriloquist was so bad his lips even moved when he wans't saying anything.

A producer is a man who gives the public what they want — and then hopes they want it.

When a chorus girl sews tiny garments, chances are she's just mending her costume.

I have a mighty peculiar contract. The first clause forbids me to read any of the others.

Show business is tough. One day they're putting your footprints in cement and the next day you're mixing it.

"Did you start out as an actor?"
"No, as a little boy."

"How did you like the show?"
"Please, not while I'm eating."

"Have you any stage experience?"
"Well, I had my leg in a cast once."

"Why do you keep applauding such a poor play?"
"To keep awake."

"Did that new play have a happy ending?"
"Sure, everybody was glad it was over."

"I heard your new play is playing to standing room only."
"Yes, nobody will buy a ticket."

"Stop acting like a fool."
"I am not acting!"

Sickness

If you have a headache, thrust your head through a window and the pane will disappear.

Anybody who can swallow an aspirin at a drinking fountain deserves to get well.

To prevent a head cold from going to your chest just tie a knot in your neck.

My wife has sinus trouble. She always says: "Sinus a check for this, sinus a check for that."

Now they have invented a remedy that cures a disease for which there is no sickness.

I've been suffering from virus X. I would have had pneumonia, but I couldn't spell it.

Get-well cards have become so humorous that nowadays if you don't get sick you're missing half the fun.

An ulcer often shows that a man is in big money: either he is making it or owing it.

The trouble with laryngitis is that you have to wait until you're cured before you can tell anybody about it.

I've been sick on my feet now for two months. I'm too strong to get sick and too weak to get well.

You're a born loser if you take a four-way cold tablet and you find out you have a five-way cold.

"Are you homesick?"
"No, I'm here sick."

"Why do you eat your dessert first?"
"My stomach is upset."

"Doctor, what should I take for my cold?"
"Don't refuse any offer."

"Honey, the doctor is here."
"Tell him I can't see him, I'm sick."

"Why is a mousetrap like the measles?"
"Because it is catching."

"What is green, has two legs and a trunk?"
"A seasick tourist."

"Have you ever caught the German measles?"
"No, I haven't even been to Germany."

"Are you taking care of your cold?"
"I've had it for weeks and it seems as good as new."

"Darling, your freckles are cute."
"Freckles, nothing. I've got the measles."

"Do you suffer from rheumatism?"
"Sure, what else can you do with it?"

"She went to Arizona for her asthma."
"Why? Couldn't she get it here?"

"Tell me, were you ever troubled with diphtheria?"
"Only when I tried to spell it."

"Why are you in such a hurry to have me cure your cold?"
"I lost my handkerchief."

Singing

I like the old songs best, because nobody sings them any more.

Nobody could sing but everybody sang.

He's not a very good singer but people like to watch his Adam's apple go up and down.

He only knows two tunes. One is Yankee Doodle and the other isn't.

When my wife sings I always stand outside on the porch. I don't want the neighbors to think I'm beating her.

Here's a boy whose songs will go to your head and to your heart – and they won't do your stomach any good either.

Old singers never die, they just lose their voices.

He would like to sing the song "The Clock" but he doesn't want to alarm anybody.

The real music lover is the woman who applauds her husband when he comes home singing at 2 a.m.

The greatest war song that was ever written is "Here Comes the Bride!"

She had a voice like a broken phonograph.

I once sang for the King of Siam. At least he told me he was. He said: "Honey, if you're a singer, I'm the King of Siam."

No, no, the song starts with "Oh say can you see?," not "Osage Kansas City."

Can she sing? She could hold a note longer than the National Bank.

She sings a lot for charity. She has to. Nobody ever offered to pay her.

They now have a new singing group – four music lovers who sing protest songs about people who only sing protest songs.

She is very stout but she sings very flat.

"Sweetheart, do you want to hear something awful?"
"No, please, don't sing!"

"I've been singing ever since I was two years old."
"No wonder you're hoarse."

"Why did the old lady put wheels on her rocking chair?"
"She wanted to rock 'n' roll."

"In what key do you sing?"
"I don't sing in a key, I sing in a night club."

"Did you notice how my voices filled the auditorium?"
"Yes, I noticed that a lot of people left to make room for them."

"Can you sing high 'C'?"
"No, I sing low-sy!"

"Sing after me; Me, me, me, me!"
"You, you, you, you!"

"I'm going away to study singing."
"Good, how far away?"

"I do all my singing in the shower."
"Don't sing very often, do you?"

"People tell me I have a rich voice."
"Well, why don't you retire it?"

"When I sing people clap their hands."
"Yes, over their ears."

"Why do you sing in the bathtub?"
"The door won't lock."

"Doesn't that soprano have a large repertoire?"
"Yes, and that dress she wears makes it look even worse."

"Don't you think I sing with feeling?"
"No. If you had any feeling, you wouldn't sing."

"Can you sing soprano?"
"Sure, if I know the words."

"Can you imagine anything worse than that solo?"
"Yes, a quartet; it's four times as bad."

"How about you and me singing a song together?"
"Okay. Let's duet."

"Did you say she sang beautifully?"
"No, I said she was a beautiful singer."

"I can sing the Star Spangled Banner for hours."
"I can sing Stars and Stripes Forever."

"They say the new prima donna is a coloratura."
"Never mind her religion. Can she sing?"

Skiing

She tried to learn how to ski, but by the time she learned how to stand, she couldn't sit down.

When going skiing, make sure you have plenty of white snow and Blue Cross.

I thought I'd take up skiing, but then I decided to let it slide.

Skiing is a wonderful sport. I spent one day skiing and six days in the hospital.

Sleeping

Everything gets easier with practice – except getting up in the morning.

I've been laying low for months. My bed sags.

The best way to cure insomnia is to get lots of sleep.

You can't fall out of bed if you sleep on the floor.

The best way to drive your wife crazy is to smile in your sleep.

Sleeping at the wheel is a good way to keep from growing old.

The woman who talks all day deserves a husband who sleeps all night.

I feel just like an Indian. Every night I sleep with a battle-axe.

The only time my wife listens to what I say is when I'm asleep.

I have to sleep in my bathing suit. My hot water bottle leaks.

I get up every morning at six a.m., no matter what time it is.

Snoring is so simple you can do it in your sleep.

My insomnia is so bad, I can't even sleep on the job.

Frequent naps prevent old age, especially when taken while driving.

I haven't slept for days. Good thing I can sleep at night.

I couldn't sleep last night. I tried counting black sheep but I couldn't see them in the dark.

I sleep fine all night and sleep all right in the morning, but all day I just toss and turn.

Counting sheep didn't help my insomnia. All it did was make me sleepy.

"Do you sleep soundly?"
"You ought to hear me."

"My doctor said I have insomnia."
"Well, don't lose any sleep over it."

"Why couldn't you wake up this morning?"
"I wasn't asleep."

"On my farm, we go to bed with the chickens."
"In our town we'd rather sleep in a bed."

"Do you wear a nightgown or pajamas?"
"No."

"Do you still walk in your sleep?"
"No, now I take carfare to bed with me."

"How did you sleep last night?"
"As usual, with my eyes closed."

"Did you wake up grumpy this morning?"
"No, I let him sleep."

"Do you always snore?"
"No, only when I'm asleep."

"Why do you take a cane to bed with you?"
"I walk in my sleep."

"Do you always sleep between two plain sheets in summer?"
"No, I sleep between the window and the door."

"Don't take your trouble to bed with you."
"But doctor, my wife won't sleep alone!"

"Do you sleep with the windows open?"
"I don't sleep with the windows at all."

"You can't sleep in my class."
"But, professor, if you'd talk a little lower I could!"

"How much sleep do you ordinarily require?"
"About five minutes more."

"How is your insomnia?"
"Worse. Can't even sleep when it is time to get up."

"Say, Harry, are you awake? There's a burglar downstairs."
"No, I'm asleep!"

Smoking

A woman is only a woman – but a good cigar is a smoke!

You've heard of cigarette lighters that don't work? Mine won't go out.

Then I became a chain smoker. I couldn't afford cigarettes.

They say smoking shortens your life. It also shortens your cigarettes.

Where there's smoke there's my wife cooking.

I haven't bought a cigarette in ten years. My brother is a street cleaner.

My wife is so neat she empties ashtrays even before they are used.

What this five cent cigar needs is a good country.

This cigar is so strong you have to knock off the ashes with a hammer.

My wife gave me a Pocket Lighter, but who wants to light pockets?

She read so much about the bad effects of smoking, she decided to stop reading.

She smokes like Chicago after the fire.

She was such a heavy smoker, when I kissed her hand I got nicotine poisoning.

It took a lot of willpower, but finally I've given up trying to give up smoking.

I know it's very easy to give up smoking. I've tried it so often.

Smoking makes a woman's voice harsh. If you don't agree, just flick some ashes on her best rug.

There are several good five-cent cigars on the market, but they are sold at higher prices.

Every time I want to smoke I have no matches.

Smokers are people who, the more they fume, the less they fret.

They now have cigarettes with ear plugs for people who don't want to hear why they should quit smoking.

The family that smokes together, chokes together.

"Sir, your car is smoking!"
"What brand?"

"Have you got a cigarette?"
"Lots of them, thanks."

"Say, mister, your car is smoking!"
"Well, it's old enough."

"Have you got a match?"
"Have I? I've got matches to burn."

"Say, your jacket is smoking."
"It's all right. It's a smoking jacket."

"Do you smoke cigarettes?"
"What else can I do with them?"

"Will you give up smoking for me?"
"Who said I'm smoking for you?"

"Darling, may I kiss your hand?"
"Sure, but don't burn your nose on my cigarette."

"How do you make a cigarette-lighter?"
"Take out the tobacco."

"Why do you roll your own cigarettes?"
"My doctor told me I needed exercise."

"How many cigarettes do you smoke a day?"
"Oh, any given amount."

"Do you care if I smoke?"
"I don't care if you burn."

"I never saw you smoke a cigar before."
"No, I just picked it up."

"I heard your wife smokes only after meals, is it true?"
"Yes, after her meal, after my meal, after everybody's meal."

"He likes cigars so much he smokes three boxes a day."
"But what does he do with the cigars?"

Soup

They call chicken soup the water they cook the eggs in.

"Waiter, get that fly out of my soup. I want to dine alone!"

"Waiter, bring me some turtle soup and make it snappy!"

He embarrassed us. He drank his soup and six couples got up and danced.

She sneezed into her tomato soup and we thought she had the measles.

You can have all the hot water you want. Just ask for soup in the dining room.

Every time my wife serves me alphabet soup the letters spell out poison.

Soup should be seen and not heard.

Listen to her eat! She's a souprano.

Never break your bread or roll in your soup.

A fly in the soup is better than no meat at all.

He's so unlucky, if it rained soup he'd have a fork.

Better to find a hair in your soup than soup in your hair.

Etiquette is the noise you don't make when you eat soup.

I had alphabet soup the other day but I couldn't eat it. My name was spelled wrong.

He always asks for alphabet soup so he can read while eating.

"This is good soup."
"Yes, it sounds good."

"This coffee is very weak."
"That's not your coffee, that's soup!"

"Waiter, this plate is wet!"
"That's your soup, sir!"

"Say, waiter, this soup tastes like dishwater."
"How do you know?"

"It looks like rain."
"It sure does, but it's chicken soup."

"Why is our waiter crying?"
"He burned his thumb in our soup."

"Waiter, this soup tastes watery."
"Wait till you taste our coffee."

"Waiter, can I have a meal on the cuff?"
"Sure, let's start with some soup in your lap."

"Say, there's a button in my soup."
"Just a little mistake. Should be mutton."

"Will you join me in a bowl of soup?"
"Do you think there's room for both of us?"

The Stock Market

I made a killing in the Stock Market. I shot my broker.

My uncle is a stock broker. That's a bloodsucker in an ivy league suit.

What keeps most people out of the Stock Market is the supermarket.

I dropped a lot of money in the market today. My shopping bag broke.

I've got some liquid assets — two bottles of whiskey.

There was a broker's wife who made her husband discharge his new secretary because she showed too much margin.

One good thing about being poor: you can read about a drop in the Stock Market without losing your appetite.

He works for a stock brokerage house called Button, Button and Zipper. Zipper replaced one of the Buttons.

It was an unusual week at the market. ATT split the same day my shopping bag did.

They are getting tough at the Stock Exchange. All seats must have seat-belts.

Now I'm in real trouble. First my laundry called and said they lost my shirt and then my broker said the same thing.

I call my dog "Broker" because he does all his trading on the curb.

Do you realize that 7-Up is down to 4 1/2?

They call him "Broker" because after you see him you are.

They now have a Stock Market doll: you wind it and it drops to the bottom.

They also have an Investor doll: you wind it and it yells "SELL!"

Wall Street is a place where the day begins with good buys.

With the present Stock Market conditions, I'm neither a bull nor a bear. I'm just a chicken.

Everything seems to go up these days, except my stock investment.

I own some stock in a company that pays quarterly dividends. Every three months they send me a quarter.

I just wish my blood pressure would go down the way my stock does.

I had a seat on the curb but the street cleaner swept me off.

I told my broker that as long as he doesn't tell me where my money should go, I won't tell him where he should go.

A street-sweeper is the only man who ever made a big cleanup on Wall Street.

"What's the latest dope on Wall Street?"
"My brother."

"That stock you sold me is worthless."
"So is the check you gave me."

"I heard your uncle lost a fortune on Wall Street."
"Yes, he dropped a quarter in a bad soda machine."

"I heard you made a lot of money in the Stock Market."
"Yes, I bought 7-up when it was only 6 1/2."

"They say there's money to be found on Wall Street."
"Good, I'll go down and look for it."

"What do you know about the bears and bulls?"
"Nothing. But I know about the birds and bees."

"I'd have to be an idiot to buy stock in your company."
"Good. How many shares do you want?"

"Put your money in oil."
"Are you crazy? Who wants oily money?"

"Why are you watering your stock certificates?"
"It's a growth stock and I hope to make it grow."

"I put half of my money in paper towels and half in revolving doors."
"I can figure out what happened. You were wiped out before you could turn around."

Subways

I just heard all the subways will get mirrors instead of windows so you can see who is pushing you around.

The subway is a wonderful thing. How else can you get to Brooklyn without being seen?

Did you know that since they put up PREVENT FOREST FIRES signs in the subway they've had no forest fires there?

No matter how conditions improve, the subway will always be in a hole.

Summer

Summer is the time when . . .

. . . children slam doors they left open all winter.

. . . it is too hot to do the jobs it was too cold to do all winter.

. . . my neighbor returns the bottle of cough medicine I loaned him and borrows my suntan lotion.

. . . people come back from their vacation to rest up on their jobs.

. . . the days get longer and the underwear shorter.

. . . there is not much on radio, TV, or the girls on the beach.

. . . they close all the roads and open the detours.

. . . you don't want to do all those things you've been wanting to do all winter.

. . you ride bumper to bumper to get to the beach, where you sit all day anyway.

. . . you try to keep your house as cold as it was in winter when you complained about it.

"Do you summer in the country?"
"No, I simmer in the city."

"What is a good thing to keep in the summer?"
"Cool."

"What is the coolest cover to use in the summer?"
"A sheet of ice."

"Why are summer days longer than winter days?"
"The heat expands them."

The Sun

When it comes to getting a suntan, ignorance is blister.

I just love sunshine. I could sit in the sun day and night.

When it's 110 in the shade, brother, don't be a dope. Stay in the sun.

The ceiling in my room was so thin, I got a sunburn and I never left the room.

Moonlight makes a girl look like a vision but in the bright sunlight she may be a sight.

He was staying up all night trying to figure out where the sun went when it went down. Finally it dawned on him.

"How did you get all those freckles on your tongue?"
"I'm always eating Swiss cheese in the sun."

"Mom, may I go out and watch the eclipse?"
"Sure, but don't stand too close."

"I got up at dawn yesterday to see the sunrise."
"Well, you couldn't have picked a better time."

"Light from the sun travels at a speed of 186,000 miles a second. Isn't it remarkable?"
"I don't know. It's downhill all the way."

"What's the idea walking around with a lit lamp?"
"I want to spread some sunshine wherever I go."

The Supermarket

. . . The only place where a housewife puts all her eggs in one basket.

. . . A convenient spot that permits a woman to go broke in one store.

. . . A place where you spend 30 minutes hunting for instant coffee.

The slowest moving item in most supermarkets is the grocery cart.

My wife found a real bargain in her supermarket. The regular 45-cent can was reduced from 85 to 77 cents.

The only time some folks follow the straight and narrow path is in the supermarket.

A young bride tried to squeeze the tomato cans in the supermarket to see if they were fresh.

The high cost of living doesn't bother me when I enter the supermarket. What gets me is the high cost of leaving!

Sweaters

I gave her something we both can enjoy: a sweater.

A sweater is a garment worn by a child when his mother feels chilly.

She was wearing a Jersey sweater and Newark never looked better.

The way girls wear sweaters nowadays, the right size is the tight size.

Sweater girls make excellent teachers. They outline things so clearly.

I gave her a three-piece sweater set for Christmas — two needles and a ball of wool.

There are two types of sweater girls: the one that knits them and the one that fits them.

A wolf is a guy who takes out a sweater girl and tries to pull the wool over her eyes.

A girl is getting old when she begins to worry more about how her shoes fit than how her sweater fits.

Sweaters come in two sizes: too large and small enough.

He cut off his arms so he could wear a sleeveless sweater.

She was wearing a sweater so tight, I could hardly breathe.

Swimming

My uncle is a swimming instructor. He gives drowning lessons.

I can swim 100 yards in two seconds — going over a waterfall.

She was only a swimming star's daughter, but she knew all the dives.

Would you call a swimming instructor a hold-up man?

Was the pool crowded? I had to dive five times before I hit water.

Many a man would like to drown his troubles but he can't get his wife to go swimming.

We even had a concrete swimming pool, but who wants to swim in concrete?

What a place! Everybody had so much fun diving into the swimming pool, they decided to put some water in.

I told my wife that if you want to learn something, you must always start at the bottom. But she wanted to learn how to swim!

They had three swimming pools: hot, cold and empty. The empty one was for people who couldn't swim.

In his back yard, he now has a big sign that says: NO LIFEGUARD ON DUTY! and underneath it says: NO SWIMMING POOL EITHER!

This swimclub is so exclusive even the tide can't get in.

He was teaching his girl how to swim when the lifeguard made them go into the water.

We couldn't afford a swimming pool so we just filled up our sunken living room with water.

"Can you swim?"
"Only in water!"

"Where did you learn how to swim?"
"In the water."

"You shouldn't be swimming on a full stomach."
"I'll swim on my back."

"Did you go swimming in the hot sun yesterday?"
"No, I went swimming in the water."

"I've eaten beef all my life and I'm now strong as an ox."
"That's funny. I've eaten fish all my life and I can't swim a stroke!"

"I heard Mike drowned last week. Couldn't he swim?"
"Sure he can. But he was a union man and it happened on his lunch hour."

T

Talking

My wife has a long-playing tongue.

A good listener is the best talker.

A woman's word is never done.

She has a tongue that could clip a hedge.

I thought talk was cheap until I saw our telephone bill.

She talks so much I get hoarse listening to her.

If you want your wife to listen, talk to another woman.

Some women are never too busy to talk about how busy they are.

She has a tongue that jaywalks over every conversation.

She has a slight impediment in her speech. She can't say no!

She is so tired at the end of the day, she can hardly keep her mouth open.

He who thinks by the inch and talks by the yard deserves to be kicked by the foot.

When a woman says "I do!" she usually knows what she's talking about.

The average woman talks 50 percent faster than her husband listens.

Confucius say: "Who say I say all those things they say I say?"

I know a woman who talks so much, last summer her tongue got sunburned.

Better to be silent and be thought a fool than to speak and remove all doubt.

I tell you, so many things have happened since I saw you last. I've had all my teeth pulled and a new stove put in.

He is not a liar; he just arranges the truth in his favor.

"I was in a jam last night."
"Tell me about it, but don't spread it too thick."

"Can you keep a straight face while telling a lie?"
"No. My lips always move."

"Do you know her to speak to?"
"No, only to talk about."

"Did you ever speak before a big audience?"
"Yes, I said 'Not guilty!'"

"So you and your wife are not speaking?"
"No, just shouting."

"I heard your wife is an after-dinner speaker."
"Don't be silly. She can't wait that long."

"What would you say if I asked you to marry me?"
"Nothing. I can't talk and laugh at the same time."

"Did you say ice cream?"
"No. You hardly speak above a whisper."

"Do you know him well enough to speak to?"
"I know him so well that I don't even talk about him."

"Do you think that women really talk more than men?"
"No, they merely use more words."

"My wife tells me I talk in my sleep, doctor. What should I do?"
"Nothing that you shouldn't."

"I'm going home to mother. I should have listened to her 20 years ago."
"Go ahead, honey. She's still talking!"

"About that habit of talking to yourself — it's nothing to worry about."
"Well, maybe not, Doctor, but I'm such an awful bore."

"Why do you have carrots sticking out of your ears?"
"Talk louder. I can't hear you. I have carrots sticking out of my ears."

"Did your wife have anything to say when you got home so late?"
"No, but it didn't stop her from talking for hours."

Taxes

She looked as good as an Income Tax refund.

I just send my income to Washington. Who can afford taxes?

I don't know why they call it pay-as-you-go. After you pay, where can you go?

An Income Tax form is like a laundry list. Either way you lose your shirt.

A fine is a tax you pay for doing wrong and a tax is a fine you pay for doing all right.

One reason that you can't take it with you is that you don't have it after taxes.

When it comes to tax reduction, never was so little waited for by so many for so long.

I keep getting threatening letters, and I wish the Tax department would stop sending them.

They wanted my tax paid in four quarters — but I gave them the dollar all at once.

Everybody tries to cheat successfully on his taxes without really lying.

When I went up to the Tax department I really let them have it — every dollar I had.

Everybody should pay his income tax with a smile. I tried it, but they wanted cash.

People who complain about their income tax are divided into two classes: men and women.

I went to Washington and visited the Tax department. I just wanted to see the people I'm working for.

They told me that they sympathize with my problems but they won't fit into the computer.

"Income Tax could be a whole lot worse. Just suppose we had to pay on what we thought we were worth!"

The new income tax form is printed in red, white and blue. When you've filled in the white, you're left in the red and that makes you blue.

"I came to talk about my taxes."
"Okay. Start lying."

"Which of your works of fiction do you consider the best?"
"My last income tax return."

Taxis

He took a taxi home every day, just to be able to tell somebody where to go.

They make a beautiful couple. She's a taxi dancer and he's a hack driver.

"It's not so much the work I enjoy," said the taxi driver, "but the people I run into."

I love to take a taxi. Too bad the meter always goes faster than the cab.

This taxi driver was having such a bad day, his flag was at half mast.

She was so bashful, she wouldn't even whistle at a taxi.

He is a man who stops at the finest hotels. He's a taxi driver.

Every time my wife gets into a taxi they leave the vacant sign up.

She was only a taxi driver's daughter, but you sure auto meter.

He's got a fine job. Goes to work in a taxi. He's a taxi driver.

"To the hospital, but don't rush. I only work there!"

Last night I had trouble with a lady taxi driver. She wanted me to sit in the back.

An eccentric cabbie is a whacky hackie.

To avoid that run-down feeling, don't walk. Take a taxi!

Taxies intend to raise the fare, but we have nothing to fear but fare itself.

They now have a Taxi Driver Doll: You wind it and it dissolves in the rain.

"What's the matter, are you blind?"
"Why? I hit you, didn't I?"

"What's the first thing that strikes you in New York City?"
"A taxi."

"Where to, sir?"
"Ten times around the park and step on it. I'm in a hurry."

"I can't stop the taxi. I lost control."
"For Heaven's sake, stop the meter!"

"Say, taxi, are you engaged?"
"No, Sir, I'm married."

Teenage

The time . . .

. . . between pigtails and cocktails.

. . . when your children begin to question your answers.

. . . when a girl makes up her face more easily than her mind.

. . . when girls begin to powder and boys begin to puff.

. . . when your child tells you the facts of life.

Teenagers

People who . . .

. . . are always ready to give adults the full benefit of their inexperience.

. . . are always ready to go buy buy.

. . . are afraid of nothing except a stack of dirty dishes.

. . . are growing up to be the kind of people their mothers didn't want them to play with.

. . . are very much alike in many disrespects.

. . . complain that there's nothing to do and then stay out all night getting it done.

. . . express a burning desire to be different by dressing exactly alike.

. . . really like homework. They can sit and look at it for hours.

. . . regard home as a drive-in where Pop pays for the hamburger.

. . . think a well-balanced diet means a hamburger in each hand. .

. . . think curbing their emotions means parking by the roadside.

. . . would rather pass their classmates on the highway than in school.

Teeth

If you can't brush after every meal – comb!

It was so cold her tooth was chattering!

Nothing is as useless as a pulled tooth!

He has Pullman teeth – one upper and one lower.

Many a true word is spoken through false teeth.

Be true to your teeth or they will be false to you!

He has teeth like the ten Commandments – all broken!

To keep your teeth in good shape mind your own business.

She has so many cavities she talks with an echo.

A person usually has three sets of teeth: temporary, permanent and false.

He reminds me of a toothache I once had!

Tough? Why, every time he stuck his tongue out he broke a tooth.

Pretty soon toothpaste will cost more than new teeth.

She had so much bridge work, every time I kissed her I had to pay a toll.

But her teeth are all her own. I was with her when she bought them.

I'd like to kick him in the teeth but why should I improve his looks?

I have so much gold in my teeth, I have to sleep with my head in a safe.

I finally broke my husband of biting his nails. I hide his teeth.

She has the brightest smile I ever saw. And last year it was even brighter when she had teeth.

He who laughs last, usually has a tooth missing.

I won't say she has big buck teeth, but the last time she used her electric toothbrush, she blew every fuse in the house.

I didn't talk for two years after I was born. I didn't want to open my mouth and let people know I had no teeth.

She has such buck teeth that every time we kissed she combed my mustache.

She was such a hot kisser she melted the gold in my teeth.

He wanted to have all his teeth pulled so he would have more gum to chew.

She has teeth like sparkling water — 7-up and one down.

She smiles so much, even her teeth are sunburned.

She is the only girl who wears her teeth parted in the middle.

Does she have buck teeth? We haven't used a bottle opener in years.

Now they have a new TV toothpaste. Comes in a 17-inch tube.

A real gourmet is a fellow who puts salt and pepper on his toothpaste.

What's new, besides your teeth?

Her teeth are so far apart, every time she opens her mouth, she looks like a picket fence.

"Why are you crying?"
"My teeth stepped on my tongue!"

"Did you lose your teeth?"
"No, I got them in my pocket!"

"I have a sweet tooth, you know."
"It looks mighty lonesome up there!"

"Do you use toothpaste?"
"What for? My teeth aren't loose."

"I'm having trouble chewing with my teeth."
"You'd have more trouble chewing without them."

"What kind of filling do you want in your teeth?"
"Chocolate, doctor!"

"Eat your spinach, dear, it makes your teeth strong."
"Why don't you give some to grandpa?"

"What has teeth but never eats?"
"A comb."

"What is the best thing out?"
"An aching tooth."

"With what instrument can you draw teeth painlessly?"
"A pencil."

"I haven't seen you in weeks. What happened?"
"Oh, I've been busy. I had a tooth taken out and a gas stove put in."

Telephone

"Pardon me, young lady. I'm writing a telephone book. May I have your number?"

He is so disagreeable, he had a phone installed just so he could hang up on people.

It's easy to tell when a woman has dialed the wrong number. She'll only talk for ten minutes.

The meanest fellow is the man who calls up the operator just to say HELLO!

He has lots of patience. He always waits for the dial tone.

He was waiting for a phone call but he couldn't wait any longer, so he left the message on the receiver.

My boss won't let me make any personal calls at the office, and my wife and daughter won't let me make them at home.

Yesterday I was talking to my girl in a phone booth but someone wanted to make a call, so we both got out.

My daughter is now at the awkward age. She knows how to make phone calls, but not how to end them.

"But, operator, the line can't be busy. I'm the only one who talks to her!"

My wife must be home. The phone is still warm.

I'm having trouble with my wife. When I'm at the office I can't get her on the phone and when I'm home I can't get her off the phone.

There was a woman who accidently got locked in a phone booth but didn't find out about it until two hours later.

My teenage daughter is very popular. The only time the phone doesn't ring is when it's for me.

I asked the waiter to bring a phone to the table but he couldn't get the booth off the wall.

Some women can talk their way out of everything but a telephone booth.

Smart? She knows 300 phone numbers by heart!

There's something wrong with our switchboard. It's full of holes.

My wife spends all day in the kitchen. She doesn't do any cooking, but that's where the phone is.

Here is a girl who accepts rings from men she doesn't even know. She's a telephone operator.

My girl wanted a flesh-colored Princess phone because it became part of her face.

A woman is a person who reaches for a chair when the phone rings.

A woman's place is in the home – usually next to the telephone.

"Is that you, darling?"
"Yes, who is calling?"

"What did you two argue over?"
"Over the telephone."

"Is my wife home?"
"No, who shall I say called?"

"What number is this?"
"You ought to know. You dialed it."

"Why are you talking backwards?"
"I dropped the dime in upside down."

"What can you give a man who has everything?"
"My phone number."

"I prayed for you last night."
"Next time telephone."

"Can kissing over the phone be fun?"
"Yes, if you are in the booth with the right girl."

"Can you telephone from a submarine?"
"Sure. Anybody can tell a phone from a submarine."

"If we become engaged, will you give me a ring?"
"Sure. What's your number?"

"How come your daughter doesn't say anything?"
"She's not used to talking until she hears the dial tone."

"I'm looking for something to give my beautiful girl."
"Well, why don't you give her my phone number?"

Television

My TV set gives me great pleasure. It keeps my wife quiet all evening.

I just bought a new color TV set. Shows only two colors: black and white.

Before TV nobody knew what stomach trouble looked like.

I was never on TV, but I was on Radar twice on the parkway.

Before retiring, take a week off and watch daytime television.

Don't believe in color TV until you see it in black and white.

TV is a medium where people with nothing to do watch people doing it.

He is ready for television. Look at his face; it's already blurred.

Some nights the only good things on TV are the vase and the clock.

A child is a thing that stands half-way between an adult and a TV set.

Television is with us to stay, if you can keep up the payments.

Television is proof that people would rather look at anything but each other.

TV's biggest problem is killing time between commercials.

There's a lot of money to be made in TV — as any repairman will tell you.

I never really believed in ghosts until I bought a television set.

Television is great. We should all be proud to go blind watching it.

We have already pay TV. I have to pay my boy 50 cents to shut it off.

I saw my repairman at the ballpark. His TV set must be broken, too.

I put a mirror on my TV set. I wanted to see what my family looked like.

I have a fine TV set. Has only two controls: my wife and my child.

I wouldn't say we have trouble with our TV set, but we now have a sleep-in repairman.

TV is a numbers game: 15-year-old movies and 24 easy payments on a 21-inch set.

My little boy likes TV better than the movies. It's not so far to the bathroom.

I won my wife on a quiz show. I didn't know the truth and she was the consequence.

I've watched so many mystery stories on TV, when I turn off the set I wipe my finger-prints off the dial.

Television will never replace the old-fashioned keyhole.

Texas

"I know my teeth are perfect, Doctor, but drill anyway. I feel lucky."

There is a hotel in Texas where, when you ring for the room service, the bellboy sends his valet up.

This Texan, unable to find a parking space for his Cadillac, gave it away and then bought one that was already parked.

In Texas you have to drop a silver dollar into the parking meter every five minutes.

You've got to admire Texas. Where else in the world do you have to be on the lookout for phony $1000 bills?

He bought a cheap radio for his friend for Christmas, but the radio was in a Cadillac.

He spent his summers in a little place he just bought up North: Canada!

After he bought some Cadillacs he said, "Well, that takes care of the Christmas cards. Now let's buy some nice presents."

"Say, my wife is sick. Do you have any get-well cars?"

Texas nursery rhyme: The butcher, the baker, the Cadillac maker.

This Texan owns an oil well that produces 500 barrels a day. Not oil, just barrels!

Thanksgiving

We're not buying a new turkey this Thanksgiving. We've still got some left over from last year.

At the Thanksgiving dinner I always get the drumsticks. Too bad I have no drum.

We are having the usual thing for our Thanksgiving dinner: relatives!

It was so chilly we had to stuff our turkey with wool instead of dressing.

I wouldn't say my wife bought a tough turkey, but we had to use an axe to cut the stuffing.

She calls her new dress "Thanksgiving" because it shows more meat than dressing.

I wouldn't say my wife didn't make a fine Thanksgiving dinner, but I was still sick on Christmas.

The way our turkey tasted, I think it was killed last Thanksgiving.

We always have to invite our relatives for the Thanksgiving dinner. We have no other choice. They bring the turkey.

The turkey was so nicely dressed I took out the turkey instead of my wife.

The turkey was so big we needed an upholsterer to stuff it.

We had a 25 lb. turkey this year, but the stuffing was almost 24 lb.

Thanksgiving is the day Mom stuffs the turkey in the morning and the family in the afternoon.

But this year I was really thankful. I didn't have to pay for the turkey.

My wife served turkey and everybody was tickled. She forgot to take off the feathers.

There is always one thing to be thankful for on Thanksgiving. Be glad you are not a turkey.

My butcher left out the stuffing in my turkey. Put the bill in instead.

We were so poor we had to stuff our turkey with newspapers.

"Did you stuff the turkey yourself?"
"I didn't have to. It wasn't hollow."

"What country is popular on Thanksgiving?"
"Turkey."

"Who's never hungry at Thanksgiving dinner?"
"The turkey. He's stuffed."

The Theater

I've always had the theater in my veins. Sometimes I wish I had blood.

She told me she was a showgirl, but she didn't have anything to show.

It was sort of a sneak preview. After ten minutes everybody sneaked out.

The show was so bad people were lined up to get out of the theater.

She has had more up and downs than a theater-goer in an aisle seat.

The critic said it was the best play in the country. The only trouble was they played it in the city.

That actor is so conceited that every time he hears a clap of thunder, he goes to the window and takes a bow.

The show was all right, but the theater was constructed poorly. All seats faced the stage.

"How're the acoustics in the new theater?"
"Splendid. The actors can hear every cough."

"Why do you keep applauding such a poor play?"
"To keep awake."

"I had to quit the theater on account of sickness."
"You mean they got sick of you?"

"Have you been seeing my new show?"
"I never miss it. I never see it and I never miss it!"

"How did you like the new show you saw last night?"
"Very refreshing. I felt like a new man when I woke up."

"What do you want to do tonight? Stay home?"
"No, I've got a bad cough. Let's go to the theater."

"I heard you have now a leading part in the theater."
"Yes, I'm the head usher."

"Sorry, you can't take that dog into the theater."
"What harm can this show do to a little dog?"

Thermometers

. . . an instrument that always has its ups and downs.

. . . an instrument that often falls but seldom breaks.

. . . an instrument that should be bought in winter because it is much higher in summer.

If your thermometer keeps dropping, use a stronger nail.

Tigers

"I wonder what that tiger would say if it could talk?"
"It would probably say: 'Pardon me, but I'm a leopard!'"

"A tiger will not harm you if you carry a white stick."
"Yes, but how fast do you have to carry this stick?"

"And while we were hunting wild animals, we saw a man-eating tiger."
"Well, some people will eat anything."

Time

The best way to save daylight is to use it.

In two days, tomorrow will be yesterday.

Never put off until tomorrow what you can put off for good.

Just when you think tomorrow will never come, it's yesterday.

He threw the clock out the window so he could see time fly.

Do you know that the night breaks and the day falls?

Time waits for no man, but it always stands still for a woman of 50.

Yesterday is experience, tomorrow is hope; today is getting from one to the other.

Enjoy yourself. These are the good old days you are going to miss in ten years.

Time may be a great healer, but it's a lousy beautician.

The best way to kill time is to get busy and work it to death.

If you think time heals everything, try sitting it out in a doctor's office.

Every time history repeats itself the price goes up.

Tongues

Some things go without saying — like her tongue.

Remember, your tongue is a wet place and likely to slip.

She got her hands all wet from holding her tongue.

Towns

I went to Philadelphia to forget. Then I went to Chicago to forget Philadelphia.

It is difficult to locate Parksville. The way they fold the road map it's in a wrinkle.

There's not much to see in a small town, but what you hear more than makes up for it.

I like this town because as soon as I get here I can go to sleep. It's the only place to go.

This town is so far from civilization, the TV sets are run by gas.

The only chance a man has of going to town is when his wife goes to the country.

"What funny names some towns have," remarked a man from Schenectady, as he read a Poughkeepsie newspaper on his way to Hackensack.

A small town is usually divided by a railroad, a main street, two churches and a lot of opinions.

"How far is the next town?"
"Oh, about five miles. You can walk it easily in an hour, if you run."

"I'm from Walla Walla."
"I heard you the first time."

Travel

I want to go where the hand of man has never set foot.

Europe is just wonderful. If you ever go there, don't miss it!

Then I went to the Arctic, where many are cold but few are frozen.

I came to see her off and she certainly was.

Travel broadens one. So do too many ice cream sodas.

Does she travel? She has been in Paris more than April.

I bought her an eight-piece traveling set: seven transfers and a dime.

No matter how far you travel, you only move two feet.

In Spain, I was looking at this fine old ruin when suddenly she winked at me.

You're from out of town? Is this a pleasure trip or do you have your wife with you?

I met my wife at the travel bureau. She was looking for a vacation and I was the last resort.

We went sightseeing until our eyes were sore. Then they showed us the sight for sore eyes.

He travels with matched luggage – two shopping bags from the supermarket.

Air travel is a way of seeing less and less of more and more.

Trips

Every time I take a trip I forget something. Last time I forgot my wife.

When my wife packs for a trip, the only thing she leaves behind is a note to the milkman.

He sure beat the system. He took a "GO NOW-PAY LATER" plan and didn't come back.

I didn't bring my wife along. It was a pleasure trip.

My wife is always talking about a trip to Europe. I have no objection – I let her talk.

I just came back from an all-expenses tour and that's what it was – all expenses.

I had a very successful trip. Found a parking space in every town.

Our tour of Europe left my wife speechless. That was the best part of the trip.

I went to a travel bureau and asked where I could go for $20. They told me.

"How did you like Venice?"
"Oh, I only stayed a few days. The whole place was flooded."

"Did you see any old ruins while traveling through Italy?"
"I had lunch with one."

"When you were in London did you see them changing the guards?"
"Were they dirty?"

"Yes, travel broadens one."
"Well, you must have been all around the world."

"How far can a spook travel?"
"From ghost to ghost."

"I heard you were in Venice. Did you see the gondolas?"
"Yes, even had lunch with one of them."

"Say, guide, are we lost?"
"We are not lost. We are here, only the trail is lost."

"Why can't you take me along on your trip?"
"Look, honey, the doctor said I should not take anything along that disagrees with me."

"That's too bad the hurricane blew your house away with your wife in it."
"That's all right. She's been wanting to take a trip for a long time anyhow."

Trouble

The best way to get into trouble is to be right at the wrong time.

The trouble with men is their trouble with women.

My neighbor has real trouble. Both his wife and his TV set aren't working.

Troubles don't bother me. I'm too busy to worry in the daytime and too sleepy to worry at night.

It is easy to handle women if you know how. The trouble is, nobody knows how!

I'm always having trouble with either my husband or my furnace. Whenever I watch one, the other goes out.

Most people who look for trouble don't know what to do when they find it.

One thing you can get without a lot of trouble is a lot of trouble.

He is a man with troubles. I think he's allergic to himself.

The trouble with the future is that it keeps getting closer and closer.

I never argue with my wife. I might win and then I would be in real trouble.

He's got troubles. Men don't trust him too far and the girls don't trust him too near.

"Do you have trouble making up your mind?"
"Yes and no!"

"My husband never goes out looking for trouble."
"No, he gets all he wants at home."

"Sir, I want to marry your daughter."
"Why tell me your troubles?"

"Guess I'll be going now. Don't trouble to see me to the door."
"It's no trouble; it's a pleasure!"

TV Dinners

Most TV Dinners taste like they have been prepared by the TV repairman.

I don't mind if my wife serves TV-Dinners — but re-runs?

She tried to warm up my TV Dinner, but the tubes got in the way.

Once they caught a fellow eating his TV Dinner in front of a radio.

My wife needs a TV repairman when she wants to serve a TV Dinner.

My wife gets frostbite serving TV Dinners.

These TV Dinners are really big business. Last night a rating service called and wanted to know what I'm eating while watching TV.

I would have a great marriage if my wife would defrost as fast as her TV dinners.

My wife has defrosted so many TV Dinners, she thinks she has experience in show business.

When I complained to my wife about her TV Dinners, she claimed that there must be something wrong with the antenna.

My wife was way ahead of her time. She served frozen dinners long before television.

My wife serves TV Dinners without the tin foil. I think she's throwing away the better part.

I've eaten so many TV Dinners that when I don't feel well I call the TV repairman.

U

Umbrellas

They say: Let a smile be your umbrella! I tried it and got a mouth full of rain.

Every morning I stay under the shower for ten minutes. Then I close my umbrella and get dressed.

If you let a smile be your umbrella, you'll be the happiest drenched person in the world.

Money saved for a rainy day buys a much smaller umbrella than it used to.

Some things are as useful as an umbrella is to a hippopotamus.

I call my umbrella "ADAM" because one of its ribs is missing.

Let a smile be your umbrella – if you like to gargle snow!

"What? You're five years old and you're not taller than my umbrella?"
"How old is the umbrella?"

"This umbrella has been in our possession for 20 years."
"That's long enough. Time to return it."

"Your umbrella looks as though it's seen better days."
"Oh, it's had its ups and downs."

"Can this fur coat be worn in the rain?"
"Lady, did you ever see a mink carrying an umbrella?"

V

Vacations

Boy, did I have a fine vacation! My wife drowned the first day.

Having a wonderful time! Wish I could afford it!

I'm taking an extended vacation: two weeks stretched out on my couch.

I'm so busy that if you see me sit down and eat, that's my vacation.

A man goes on vacation to wear out his old clothes while a woman goes to show off her new ones.

His idea of a vacation is to rest in the shade of a beautiful blonde.

We had a wonderful vacation. Went through five states, ten cities and 85 toll booths.

Poison ivy! Mosquito bites! Scratches! If I didn't need a vacation so badly, I would have gone home.

I like to wander around. Actually, I never got lost, but I was bewildered for three days.

He gets two vacations a year: when his son goes to camp and when his wife goes to Florida.

He has just two weeks to live because at the end of that time his wife will be back from her vacation.

If you can't get away for a vacation, you can get the same feeling by staying home and tipping every second person you see.

One of today's mysteries is why it takes four-weeks' salary to pay for a two-week vacation.

People go on vacation to forget things and when they open their suitcases find out they did.

A girl has a choice: she can go to the mountains and see the scenery or go to the beach and *be* the scenery.

The only book that really tells you where you can go on your vacation is your checkbook.

There are two kinds of people this time of the year: those who are broke, and those who haven't taken their vacation yet.

I slept a whole week in a sewer. It was the only place I could get a room with running water.

The way some women pack for a trip, the only thing they leave behind is a note for the milkman.

A short vacation is half a loaf.

People always try to fit a long vacation into a short bankroll.

Some people take their vacation late in the season to avoid the rush of people taking their holidays early in the season to avoid the rush.

"Does your vacation start soon?"
"Yes, my wife is leaving tomorrow."

"Did you find it expensive at the seashore?"
"Very. Even the tide was high."

"What kind of time did you have in New York?"
"Eastern Standard Time."

"What was your biggest vacation expense?"
"My wife."

"Where did you go on your vacation?"
"I won't know until my films are developed."

"So you are just back from vacation. Feel any change?"
"Not a penny."

"When you go to Yellowstone Park, don't forget Old Faithful."
"I'm taking her with me."

"You're certainly kind to send your wife away for a rest."
"Yes, and God knows I need it."

"When you sailed around Italy, did you touch Florence?"
"No, her husband was home."

"I think I left the electric iron on when we left in a hurry."
"Don't worry, I'm sure I left the water running, so everything will be all right."

"How much vacation will I get here?"
"A month. Two weeks when the boss goes on vacation and two weeks when you go."

W

Waiters and Waitresses

"Waiter, would you bring me a smaller check?"

A waitress is not the tomato that comes with the 50-cent salad.

A headwaiter is usually the best-dressed man in a restaurant.

Every time I pinch a waitress I see flying saucers.

I've got all the girls eating out of my hand: I'm a waiter!

This place has tip-top waiters. If you don't tip they blow their top.

The world's best after dinner speech: "Waiter, I'll take both checks!"

An excited waiter will give you nervous service.

When I asked the waiter for a corner table, I got one. At the corner of 3rd Avenue and 47th Street

"Waiter, take back the ice cream. It's cold!"

"Now I've spilled the beans," said the waiter, as he spilled the beans.

A New York man claims to have gone 44 days without food. He should have given his order to another waiter.

A man is getting along in years when he pays more attention to the food than he does to the waitress.

I've never seen such waiters. When you eat alphabet soup they read over your shoulders.

He flirted with the waitress. He was playing for bigger steaks.

They have now a headwaiter doll: you wind it up and it looks the other way.

A waiter is a man who finally comes to him who waits.

The only waiter who never accepts a tip is a dumbwaiter.

"Say, waiter, what was the dish I just ate?"
"I don't know. I'm a stranger here myself."

"Waiter, I'm so hungry I could eat a horse."
"You couldn't have come to a better place, sir."

"Say, waiter, what time is it?"
"Sorry, sir, this isn't my table."

"Say, waiter, is the food here good?"
"I don't know, sir. I never eat here!"

"How would you like your rice, Miss?"
"Thrown at me!"

"We have everything on the menu today, sir."
"So I see. Bring me a clean one."

"Say, waiter, what's good to eat?"
"Candy bars, but they will spoil your appetite."

"Say, waiter, how is the food here?"
"I'm only a waiter, not a witness."

"Say, waiter, where is your menu?"
"The second door to the right."

"Say, waiter, is this chicken or veal pie?"
"Whichever you ordered, sir."

"Say, waiter, do you serve a balanced diet?"
"Sure, our food has never fallen off the tray yet!"

"Say, waiter, where is the washroom?"
"This is no place to do your laundry."

"Say, waiter, this water is cloudy."
"The water is okay, sir. Just the glass is dirty."

"Say, waiter, these beets taste like radishes."
"That's probably because they're radishes!"

George Washington

If George Washington was such a busy man, when did he find time to build his bridge?

I'm sure George Washington was not a sailor, because anybody who stands up in a rowboat is not a sailor.

I finally found out why Washington was standing up in that boat. Every time he sat down, someone handed him an oar.

If George Washington were alive today he'd be most noted for his old age.

"It's Washington's birthday so I baked a cherry pie."
"All right, honey. Bring me a hatchet so I can cut it!"

"My father has a George Washington watch."
"That's nothing. My Dad has an Adam's apple."

'What did Washington say before crossing the Delaware?"
"Get in the boat, men."

"Why was Washington buried in Mt. Vernon?"
"Because he was dead."

"Now tell me, in what year did George Washington die?"
"Die? I didn't even know he was sick."

"Why do we always celebrate Washington's birthday?"
"Because it's a holiday."

"This country is sure progressing."
"Sure is. George Washington couldn't tell a lie. Now everybody can."

Watches

My gold watch has an excellent movement – to and from the pawn shop.

A watch is something a woman uses to see how late she is.

A watchmaker has managed to make some of his watches go so fast they get 14 days in a week.

He bought a waterproof watch. It is guaranteed that any water that leaks in won't ever leak out.

There's something wrong with my watch. One hand doesn't know what the other is doing.

Every time I ask someone what time it is, I get a different answer.

I now have a wonder watch. Every time I look at it I wonder what time it is.

My watch is on the bum. My husband wears it.

I left my watch upstairs and it ran down.

There's only one trouble with this watch. It doesn't tell time. You have to look at it.

My uncle is in the watch business. I work and he watches.

A man lost his watch and found it five blocks away. The watch was still running when he found it.

"Is this a second-hand store? I want one for my watch."

The best way to tell time by the sun is to shade your eyes and look at your watch.

A watchmaker is a man who is always working over time.

Did you hear about the man who had a waterproof, shockproof, unbreakable, anti-magnetic watch and he lost it?

I can work the whole day without looking at the clock. I've got a wrist watch.

He wears his girl's picture in his watch case because he thinks he will learn to love her in time.

He wrapped his watch in cellophane to keep the ticks out of his pocket.

He took his watch apart to see what makes it tick.

He put his watch on a scale, to see if it was gaining time.

"Are you a clock watcher?"
"No, I work outdoors. I'm a whistle listener."

"Your watch is sure sick looking."
"Yes, because it's hours are numbered."

"How do you like your new watch?"
"It's terrific! If I wind it fully it does an hour in 55 minutes."

"I once ate a watch."
"Wasn't that time-consuming?"

"Why do you carry two watches?"
"I need one to see how slow the other one is."

"How can you make money selling watches so cheap?"
"Easy, we make a profit repairing them."

"I heard you were arrested for stealing a watch."
"That's right. The lawyer got the case and the judge gave me the works."

"I wonder what time it is? I'm invited to dinner at 8:30 and my watch isn't going."
"Why? Wasn't your watch invited?"

Water

I've been in hot water so often, I feel like a teabag.

Every time I wash ice cubes in hot water, I can't find them!

Water is used more often for making oceans than for anything else.

Always getting into hot water will cook your goose.

The best way to keep your daughter out of hot water is to put some dishes in it.

Water kills more people than liquor. Remember the flood?

What's so wonderful about the ocean? After all, if you have seen one, you've seen them all!

He always wore pumps because he had water on the knees.

"I hope I made myself clear!" said the water as it passed through the filter.

I never drink water. I'm afraid it could become habit-forming.

A glass of water can sure excite you, especially when your wife spills it on you while you are sleeping.

"Say, look at all that water in that lake."
"Yeh, and that's only the top of it."

"Do you have hot water in your house?"
"We sure do, and I'm always in it."

Weather

The weather here is different. It's the only place where you get a sunburn right over your frostbite.

I used to be a weatherman, but then my corns healed up.

Weatherman on the phone: "My corns hurt too, madam, but we still say it will be clear and sunny."

In Hawaii, where the weather is the same the year around, we wonder how they start conversations?

A weatherman is a man who can look in a girl's eye and tell whether.

The forecast for tomorrow should read: partly cloudy, partly sunny, partly accurate.

Weather forecast: Friday dew, Saturday dew, Sunday don't.

It's so foggy here that on a clear day you can see the fog.

It was so foggy out I couldn't see what the weather was like.

It seems as though the weather this year has been more unusual than the usual unusual weather.

No matter how hot it is in New York City, you can always go to a night club and when they hand you the check it will knock you out cold.

She walked around on the street with her purse open, because they were expecting some change in the weather.

Hot weather never bothers me. I just drop the thermometer out the window and watch the temperature drop.

"How did you find the weather while you were away?"
"I just went outside and there it was."

"Remember, it was a storm like this the night you declared your love to me."
"Yes, it was a terrible night."

"My doctor told me today I need a change of climate."
"That's fine. According to the weather report, it's coming tomorrow."

"Shut the door, it's cold outside."
"Will that make it warmer outside?"

Weddings

A wedding usually means showers for the bride and curtains for the groom.

After paying for the wedding, about all a father has left to give away is the bride.

The best way for a woman to preserve her wedding ring is to dip it in dishwater three times a day.

I had so much fun at my bachelor party I postponed the wedding.

Did you hear about the bride who was so pleased with her wedding that she could hardly wait for her next one?

There was this good little girl who has been saying "No" so long she almost messed up her wedding ceremony.

When the preacher says "For better or for worse" it means the groom couldn't do better and the bride couldn't do worse.

The wedding cake is the only cake which, once eaten, can give you indigestion for the rest of your life.

She went to the altar with her hair in rollers because she wanted to look nice for the reception.

While passing the collection plate at a church wedding the usher said: "Yes madam, I know it's unusual, but the father of the bride requested it."

"Have I told you about my daughter's wedding?"
"No, and I appreciate it."

"Are you a friend of the groom?"
"Indeed no. I'm the bride's mother."

"Is it unlucky to postpone a wedding?"
"Not if you keep postponing it."

"Was that a big wedding you went to yesterday?"
"And how! I got in line to kiss the bride three times and nobody saw me."

Wives

I would never buy an encyclopedia. My wife knows everything.

I wouldn't say my wife is smart, but her I.Q. is 20:20.

I'd like to buy some flowers for the woman I love, but my wife won't let me.

I'll never forget our wedding. I've tried to but my wife won't let me.

I'm a married man and I can't ask for a better wife — but I would like to.

I'm always kidding about my wife, but everytime I introduce her to anybody they say: "You must be kidding!"

If your wife doesn't treat you as she should — be thankful!

Is he henpecked? He's still taking orders from his first wife.

Isn't it amazing how easy it is for a man to understand a wife, when she isn't his?

It's amazing what my wife would rather have than money.

"Does your wife miss you much?"
"No, she throws remarkably straight for a woman."

"What's the first thing your wife does when she gets up in the morning?"
"She sharpens her tongue."

"Where have you been so late?"
"Stop me, honey, if you've heard this one."

"Who introduced you to your wife?"
"We just met. I can't blame anyone."

"Waiter! My wife just dropped dead."
"Chef! There is something wrong again with the mushrooms!"

"Is your wife outspoken?"
"Not by anyone I know of."

"What do you and your wife fight about all the time?"
"I don't know. She won't tell me."

"What makes you think your wife is getting tired of you?"
"She keeps wrapping my lunch in roadmaps."

Wind

I blew into town yesterday. Strong wind!

"Do me a favor. Make like a hurricane and blow!"

The wind was so strong it blew out three fuses.

"Now it all comes back," said the skunk when the wind changed.

Winter

Winter is the season that's so cold, even the wind howls about it.

Winter is the season when you try to keep your house as hot as it was all summer.

I don't mind Spring, Summer or Fall, but Winter leaves me cold.

Winter must be here. My car heater won't work.

Winter: stuff that rich people go south during.

Women

No woman has ever shot her husband while he was doing the dishes.

When a woman is looking for a husband she is either single or married.

The only woman who can make me wish to be single again is my wife.

No woman makes a fool out of a man. She only directs the performance.

There are two ways to handle a woman and both are wrong.

Give a woman an inch and she thinks she is a ruler.

The upkeep of women is the downfall of men.

There are three kinds of women: the intelligent, the beautiful, and the majority.

A truthful woman is one who won't lie about anything except her age, weight and her husband's salary.

Running after women never hurt anybody. It's the catching that does the damage.

There are two kinds of women: the kind you dream about and the kind you marry.

There is only one bad woman in the world and every husband thinks she is his wife.

The reason so many women of 40 have so many aches and pains is because most of them are 50.

There are only two men in the world that understand women. One is dead and the other is crazy.

"No woman ever made a fool of me."
"Who did then?"

"Which would you rather give up, wine or women?"
"It depends on the vintage."

"I heard they now make bread out of potatoes."
"That's nothing. Women can make monkeys out of men."

"Do you mean to tell me you don't fool around with women?"
"That's not what I said. I said, when it comes to women, I don't fool around."

Women Drivers

When a woman driver gives you half of the road it's usually on both sides of her.

If you don't like the way women drive, get off the sidewalk!

My wife backed the car out of the garage but she forgot she backed in it the night before.

After a woman parks her car she has only a short walk to the sidewalk.

After a woman parks her car she has to decide which of the two meters to use.

Nothing confuses a man more than a woman driver who does everything right.

When two cars are double-parked, the one parked by a woman is the one on top.

She has been stopped so often by traffic cops they finally gave her a season ticket.

"Gee, dad. I wish you would let Mom drive. It's more exciting!"

She is a careful driver. Always slows down when passing a red light.

Attention everybody: my wife has the car!

We bumped into some friends yesterday. My wife was driving.

She is an excellent driver. She only has trouble with starting, stopping, turning and parking.

Does she know how to drive? She just got a ticket for making a U-turn in the Lincoln Tunnel.

Work

Work is a fine thing if it doesn't take up too much of your spare time.

The best way to keep your job is to get things mixed up the first day you're on the job so the boss can't fire you.

Story of a failure: hired, tired, fired.

Who says nothing is impossible? I've been doing nothing for years.

Work faithfully eight hours a day, and don't worry. In time you will become the boss and work 12 hours a day and do all the worrying.

Robinson Crusoe started the 40-hour work week. He had all the work done by Friday.

When it comes to work, there are many who will stop at nothing.

Ever since he was old enough to work, he didn't.

Ideas are funny, they won't work unless you do.

These days, if you want to relax you really have to work for it.

I am not afraid of hard work. Why, I could go to sleep right beside it.

I like the job; it's the work I hate.

I like work; it fascinates me. I can sit and look at it for hours.

I'm working on big things now. I'm crossing limburger with chlorophyll.

I may get to work late, but I make it up by leaving early.

I never worked a day in my life. I'm a night watchman.

I used to be a white-collar worker. But I had to quit. The collar got dirty.

"And here we see a skyscraper."
"Oh, I would love to see it work."

"How many people work in your office?"
"Oh, about half."

"I heard Jim now works as a baker."
"I guess he kneads the dough."

"What time do you start to work?"
"Oh, about two hours after I get there."

"Whom are you working for?"
"Same people. My wife and four kids."

"How long have you been working here?"
"Ever since the boss threatened to fire me."

"How long have you been out of work?"
"I don't know. I lost my birth certificate."

"Where is a good place to go when you are broke?"
"Go to work."

"I hear you've been coming to work late every day."
"Yes, boss, but I go home early."

"I understand you have something here that doesn't work?"
"Yes, he is lying on the couch sleeping."

"Why do you wear dark glasses in your house?"
"I can't see my wife working so hard."

"I wish you wouldn't whistle while you work?"
"But boss, who's working?"

The World

My wife wanted to see the world, so I bought her an atlas.

If it is a small world, why does it cost so much to run it?

We have the highest standard of living in the world. Too bad we can't afford it.

When the world is round, how can you travel to the four corners of it?

At first we thought the world was flat. Next we decided it was round. Today we know it is crooked.

It's a small world — until you chase your hat down the street.

In this world, you gotta be crazy or you'll go nuts.

If the world is getting smaller, how come it takes me longer to drive to work?

The world is getting so dangerous, it isn't safe anymore to be alive.

The whole world is a pressure cooker and nobody knows if the safety valve works.

"I would go to the end of the world for you!"
"Yes, but would you stay there?"

"What do you do when all the world is gray and gloomy?"
"I deliver the milk."

"Darling, you're all the world to me."
"Well, I still won't let you go on a sightseeing tour."

Writing

I'm having my typewriter fixed. This O is upside down.

I will have to buy a new typewriter. This one makes too many mistakes.

Every time I have some ideas I have no pencil.

"You write? What a coincidence. I read!"

Most poets will tell you that rhyme doesn't pay.

No matter how you move it, writing paper remains stationery.

He cut his fingers off so he could write shorthand.

"Everything he writes is no good."
"I know. I tried to cash his check."

"Why is it bad to write on an empty stomach?"
"Because paper is better."

"I wonder who this telegram is from?"
"Western Union. I recognize the handwriting."

"Why do you write so slow?"
"I'm a slow reader."

"Who writes the most letters?"
"A fisherman. He always drops a line."

"So you're writing a down-to-earth story?"
"Yes, it's about a parachute jumper."

"I have only a verbal contract."
"But a verbal contract isn't worth the paper it is written on."

"Can you do anything that other people can't?"
"Sure, I can read my own handwriting."

"I heard your son is a writer. Does he write for money?"
"Yes, in every letter we get."

"What is a proper place for a proof-reader?"
"The house of correction."

Y

Youth

The best way for a girl to keep her youth is not to introduce him to anyone.

The best way to recapture your youth is to take the car keys away from him.

I think every girl should hold on to her youth, but not while he's driving.

Some folks spend their youth thinking how to spend their youth.

Z

The Zoo

"Have you been to a zoo? I mean as a visitor?"

Every time she went to the zoo she had to buy two tickets. One to get in and one to get out.

Well, I have to be off to the zoo now. I have to pick up some Christmas seals.

Good Housekeeping has more seals than the Bronx Zoo.

"When I was seven years old my father took me to the zoo."
"Were you accepted?"

"Why don't you take junior to the zoo?"
"Nothing doing! If they want him, let them come and get him!"

Reference Guide

Reference Guide